Achieving Equity & Excellence

Immediate Results From the Lessons of High-Poverty, High-Success Schools

DOUGLAS REEVES

Solution Tree | Press
a division of
Solution Tree

555 North Morton Street
Bloomington, IN 47404
800.733.6786 (toll free) / 812.336.7700
FAX: 812.336.7790

email: info@SolutionTree.com
SolutionTree.com

Printed in the United States of America

Library of Congress Cataloging-in-Publication Data

Names: Reeves, Douglas B., 1953- author.
Title: Achieving equity and excellence : immediate results from the lessons
of high-poverty, high-success schools / Douglas Reeves.
Description: Bloomington, IN : Solution Tree Press, [2019] | Includes
bibliographical references and index.
Identifiers: LCCN 2019024086 (print) | LCCN 2019024087 (ebook) | ISBN
9781949539431 (paperback) | ISBN 9781949539448 (ebook)
Subjects: LCSH: Educational equalization. | Academic achievement. |
Low-income students. | Educational accountability. | School improvement
programs.
Classification: LCC LC213 .R44 2019 (print) | LCC LC213 (ebook) | DDC
379.2/6--dc23
LC record available at https://lccn.loc.gov/2019024086
LC ebook record available at https://lccn.loc.gov/2019024087

Solution Tree
Jeffrey C. Jones, CEO
Edmund M. Ackerman, President

Solution Tree Press
President and Publisher: Douglas M. Rife
Associate Publisher: Sarah Payne-Mills
Art Director: Rian Anderson
Managing Production Editor: Kendra Slayton
Production Editor: Alissa Voss
Content Development Specialist: Amy Rubenstein
Copy Editor: Evie Madsen
Proofreader: Sarah Ludwig
Text and Cover Designer: Laura Cox
Editorial Assistant: Sarah Ludwig

For Amy and Mary

Acknowledgments

My debts are too numerous to mention, but I will nevertheless attempt at least a few. To Rick and Becky DuFour, for their friendship, challenging intellect, and standard of excellence, which guide me daily to be a better teacher, leader, and writer. To Robert Eaker, for a model of friendship and intellectual rigor—he is what I want to be when I grow up. To the Solution Tree team, with whom I have collaborated for close to two decades—Jeff Jones, chief executive officer, and Douglas Rife, publisher, exemplify what partnership means, consistently elevating the interests of the teachers, leaders, and students whom they serve above short-term business considerations. Alissa Voss provided detailed and constructive feedback that made this a better book than if it had been left to my efforts alone.

I owe a special intellectual debt to Karin Chenoweth, for whom footnotes and reference citations are woefully inadequate recognitions of her seminal contribution to the scholarship of success in high-poverty schools. Robert Pondiscio writes with courage and eloquence, and challenges everyone who researches and writes about equity and excellence to put ourselves in the shoes of students and parents. Anthony Muhammad and Luis Cruz have influenced my understanding of the role of culture in schools of every socioeconomic status. Michael Fullan reminds me that fundamental truths in education transcend time and international boundaries. My colleagues at Creative Leadership Solutions have been my friends and intellectual inspirations. They include Lisa Almeida, Kate Anderson Foley, Brandon Doubek, Tony Flach, Lauren Mahoney, Kim Marshall, Brian McNulty, Stacy Scott, Mike Wasta, and many others. Special thanks to Allison Wedell, whose assistance in research and editing were vital to the completion of this book. To Julie Reeves who, in her 96th year, continues to research and write original papers on Abraham Lincoln, tend her garden, provide love and encouragement for generations of family and friends, and model the admonition of Saint Augustine to preach the Gospel at all times and when necessary, use words; her every act of kindness and generosity is worth a lifetime of sermons.

While I am happy to share credit, I do not share blame for the inevitable errors, omissions, and other failures. The only worse thing than failing to publish is to publish and then be held to public account for these mistakes, a burden I happily accept alone.

—Douglas Reeves, Boston, Massachusetts

Solution Tree Press would like to thank the following reviewers:

Carrie Barnett
Instructional Coach
San Jacinto Unified School District
San Jacinto, California

Jonathan Cornue
Staff and Curriculum Development
Madison-Oneida Board of Cooperative
  Educational Services
Verona, New York

Michael Giromini
Principal
Royal Oak High School
Royal Oak, Michigan

Andy Pattee
Superintendent
Cedar Falls Community School District
Cedar Falls, Iowa

Brad Randmark
Assistant Principal
Burnham School
Cicero, Illinois

Table of Contents

About the Author

Douglas Reeves, PhD, is the author of more than thirty books and many articles about leadership and organizational effectiveness. He was named the Brock International Laureate for his contributions to education and received the Contribution to the Field Award from the National Staff Development Council (now Learning Forward). Dr. Reeves was twice named to the Harvard University Distinguished Authors Series. Dr. Reeves has addressed audiences in all fifty U.S. states and more than thirty countries, sharing his research and supporting effective leadership at the local, state, and national levels. He is founder of Finish the Dissertation, a free and noncommercial service for doctoral students, and the Zambian Leadership and Learning Institute. He is the founding editor and co-publisher of *The SNAFU Review,* a collection of essays, poetry, and art by disabled veterans. Dr. Reeves lives with his family in downtown Boston.

To learn more about the work of Dr. Reeves, visit Creative Leadership Solutions at https://creativeleadership.net, or follow @DouglasReeves on Twitter.

To book Douglas Reeves for professional development, contact pd@SolutionTree.com.

Introduction

Allow me to offer a conjecture about you as the reader of this book. Your interest in student equity and excellence is not passive, as you have a personal and professional interest in seeing more students succeed. You have lost patience with solutions offering long-term results when the students you encounter need results *right now.* You are weary of commercial programs that "worked" with a group of students far, far away, but have been ineffective with your students. And you are impatient with the rhetoric of blame and excuses that serve only to remove the sense of urgency you know is essential to help the students you serve. You may be an educational leader, teacher, parent, or policymaker, but whatever your role, you have a deep sense of responsibility for the children from your own home and those from homes you may never visit but which are, nevertheless, part of the fabric of a society that can be far more just and equitable. If any of these descriptions fit you, please read on.

This book aims to improve the results of all students in your school, no matter their background or socioeconomic status, from the moment you begin applying the principles in the following chapters. This book offers no long-term, five-year plans for success, but rather, examples of how students can make dramatic improvements in achievement, behavior, and attendance in a single semester. You will find a methodology not based on faraway research, but on identifying, documenting, and replicating the results in your school and your community. The local and relevant evidence can be replicated within your budget, your bargaining agreement, and your community's culture. You will find no rhetoric of blame, but rather the promise of hope that tomorrow will be better than today because you already know what to do, right here, right now, without changes in state or local policy. You will find a proven change methodology that does not rely on the traditional and discredited philosophy of *persuasion before action.* You will find the fundamental truth that action—not studies, not rhetoric, not leadership charisma, but *action*—is what leads to change that works. That is inside-out change, based on modeling from successful students, teachers, and schools all within your own neighborhood.

The fundamental argument of this book is that equity and excellence must be dual goals for every school, not mutually exclusive goals in which the pursuit of equity is the mirage laid in front of schools serving high populations of students in poverty, and excellence is the exclusive province of schools serving students in wealthy suburbs or elite private schools. As Robert Pondiscio (2019) explains:

> The last several decades of education policy have set equity and excellence at war with each other. If you are wealthy, with the means to pay tuition or move to a community with great schools, you have ready access to excellence. If you are poor, black, or brown, you get equity and an impotent lecture: on fairness, on democracy, or, infuriatingly, on the need for patience and restraint. (p. 322)

Anthony Muhammad and Luis F. Cruz (2019) similarly make the case that the path to change is culture, not rhetorical flourishes or the displacement of rigor with sympathy, that creates an environment of high expectations for every student, providing to the poorest students in urban and rural areas the same climate and culture to which their suburban counterparts are routinely exposed.

Although there are certainly unique elements to every school and every child, that does not justify the inconsistent chaos in leadership, pedagogy, and curriculum that pervades many schools and, in particular, schools serving students from low-income families. The synthesis of the research in these pages is that we can and must simultaneously honor and value the individual chrematistics of each child, while also providing the results that effective culture, expectations, feedback, teaching, and leadership provide. Such dual pursuit of equity and excellence is rarely a required change for wealthy schools. However, it is a clarion call to action in the schools serving the poor, brown, and black children who are the focus of this book.

Introduction to Equity and Excellence Schools

To improve excellence for all while maintaining equity for all, the principles and strategies in this book reflect those practices that high-poverty, high-achieving schools adopt. I refer to these schools as *equity and excellence schools.* The term *equity and excellence schools* is based on systematic observations of schools with the characteristics in the following list. In my original research (Reeves, 2004) that began in the 1990s, I identified a set of *90/90/90 schools*, or schools in which:

- 90 percent or more of students qualify for free or reduced-price lunch

- 90 percent or more of students are members of ethnic or linguistic minority groups

- 90 percent or more of students pass state assessments (as defined by the various jurisdictions of the schools)

Since that original research, I have expanded my inquiry and, as the following pages make clear, benefitted from the research of many other people whose fields of inquiry included successful high-poverty schools. Therefore, for the purposes of this book, I have replaced the term *90/90/90 schools* with *equity and excellence schools* in order to convey more accurately the broad scope of schools that are described in these chapters.

The original equity and excellence studies (Reeves, 2004) focused on 135 schools in Milwaukee, Wisconsin. This research was undertaken by my colleagues and me at the Center for Performance Assessment in the course of our support for a comprehensive accountability system in what was then one of the nation's largest school districts with more than 104,000 students. For most of those 135 schools, there was a clear relationship between higher poverty rates and lower levels of achievement. But there were a few outliers—schools with both high poverty and high achievement. This allowed me to make a careful comparison between the practices of the high-achieving schools and those that were lower achieving. Because all schools in this initial study were in the same district, the variables often associated with student performance—per-pupil funding, teacher assignment policies, and union bargaining agreements—were all the same for both high- and low-performing schools. Therefore, the differences in student performance were not related to these external factors but rather to differences in professional practices by teachers and administrators.

We conducted field interviews and observations with principals and teachers throughout the district in order to better understand the leadership and teaching practices that distinguished the high-performing, high-poverty schools from their lower-performing counterparts. In addition, we collected data from each school not only on state test scores but also on school-based professional practices, such as nonfiction writing, collaborative scoring, and so on. The result is the professional practices I recommend in part II (page 29) of this book. My colleagues and I are confident that these professional practices had made the difference because all the schools compared, whether high- or low-achieving, had the same per-pupil funding, union agreement, teacher assignment policy, and board policies.

In subsequent years, this small group of outlier schools tripled in size from the original seven schools to more than twenty schools—again without changes in budget, bargaining agreement, teacher assignment policy, or board policies. Then other researchers (Chenoweth, 2009, 2017, 2019; Education Trust, n.d.; Womack, Moore, & Hill-Cunningham, 2018; Zavadsky, 2009) found similar results, identifying similar practices that made critical improvements in student achievement. Other recent research supporting high performance in high-poverty schools includes work by Karin Chenoweth and Christina Theokas (2011); Susan Moore Johnson, Stefanie K. Reinhorn, and Nicole S. Simon (2018); Sarah McKibben (2018); Jim Paterson (2018); Michael J. Petrilli (2019); and Robert Slavin (2019a, 2019b). Although each of these researchers operated independently, all came to the strikingly similar conclusion—success is possible in high-poverty schools, and these successes can be replicated on a large scale. It is important to note none of these studies find a commercial program led to the increase in student achievement; rather, the difference was dependent on the daily decisions of teachers and leaders.

In This Book

This book is divided into four parts. Part I delves into the questions that you, as educators and school leaders, must ask when presented with potential change initiatives for your schools (namely, "Do I trust this research?"). Chapter 1 explains how not all research is equal and describes five different levels of educational research that form the basis of change proposals. Savvy readers must be able to sort the wheat from the chaff when it comes to educational research and select those changes the evidence most supports for implementation in their schools. Once you select a change initiative, chapter 2 deals with the inevitable objections that will arise. This chapter uses the example of equity and excellence schools to demonstrate how leaders may respond to such resistance to change, and explains why you, as readers, can trust the equity and excellence research.

Part II presents the results of the equity and excellence research by devoting one chapter to each of the seven teaching and leadership practices that distinguish equity and excellence schools from similar schools with lower performance. According to the research, equity and excellence schools do the following (Reeves, 2004).

1. Organize their school or district as a professional learning community (PLC)

2. Display a laser-like focus on student achievement

3. Conduct collaborative scoring

4. Emphasize nonfiction writing

5. Utilize frequent formative assessment with multiple opportunities for success

6. Perform constructive data analysis

7. Engage in cross-disciplinary units of instruction

When you establish these practices in your own schools and districts, you are likely to see improved achievement for all students within a single school year.

The challenge of part III is to move from research to practice. In this section, you will consider how to apply the equity and excellence research in any school. This section will discuss the equity and excellence mindset and its differences from prevailing mindset theories, and introduce the key implementation model of *behavior precedes belief* to help teachers and leaders break free of the bonds of traditional change models. Part III also discusses the importance of transforming vision into action through promoting teacher leadership, and how to improve coaching, feedback, and evaluation methods throughout schools and districts.

Part IV returns to the roots of the equity and excellence research by advocating for the development of an accountability system that will help any school system (large or small) identify, document, assess, and replicate successful strategies. It discusses the importance of accountability indicators, from the system level to the school and department levels, as well as the necessity of an accompanying narrative for stakeholders to more fully explain the story behind the numbers.

The book concludes with a clarion call for giant leaps, not baby steps. This is not the time for the meek and tentative.

In the pages that follow, you will find all the tools you need to be bold and to forge ahead with confidence because the students you serve deserve nothing less than your courage, resilience, and perseverance.

A Word About Sources

The extensive reference section acknowledges the work of many scholars in this field, and I hope that I have done them justice. I have found a great deal of commonality among their writings and also a strong sense of consistency with my own research. I have also included observations from the field and, where possible, named the people, schools, and districts involved. In other cases, I have used a synthesis of observations and my conclusions from my work in fifty states and more than thirty countries. These observations and conclusions represent my best thinking on the matter in late 2019, but I acknowledge that much research remains to be done. Where there is a relevant citation of the work of others, I have included it to the best of my ability. The conclusions without citations represent my observations from extensive research and field study over more than twenty-five years.

PART I

Discovering When to Trust Educational Research

Our journey begins as every educational decision must—with evidence. Since publication of the original research on equity and excellence schools (Reeves, 2004), there have been two competing narratives about the influence of poverty on student achievement. The first and dominant narrative is that *demography is destiny*. This is an echo of American sociologist, theorist, and empirical researcher James S. Coleman's (Coleman et al., 1966) report, *Equality of Educational Opportunity*, which contends that the strongest predictor of student academic success is the mother's level of education. From the 1960s through the early years of the 21st century, the assertion that schools with high percentages of low-income students who are members of ethnic minorities and do not speak English at home would inevitably have low achievement seemed incontrovertible. Whenever there were *outliers*—that is, schools with students from low-income families who performed well academically—these schools stood out because they were so unusual. This narrative remains dominant in North American education. When I present data to the contrary—that not only individual schools but also entire districts are defying the odds—some educators and administrators may challenge the accuracy and credibility of the data. Even when I present data from their own districts and schools, there remains hard-core disbelief in the notion that poor children and children of color can succeed in the American educational system.

In my keynotes, seminars, and personal conversations across the United States and around the world, I often ask, "Why do teachers and administrators distrust educational research?" The answers include the following.

- The research doesn't apply to us. We are different because we are urban (or rural or suburban), our union contract is different, our budget is different, and our parents are different.

- The research has a tiny sample size that cannot be generalized to the broader student population.

- The research is from schools with heroic teachers and administrators, but they will burn out because their efforts are unsustainable.

- The research is commercially tainted because publishers conduct it while attempting to sell their textbooks, online systems, or instructional programs.

- The criteria for success are too low, so what the research calls *meeting standards* is not equivalent to what our district regards as a successful outcome.

- The per-pupil funding in the research is higher than in our schools.

- The successful schools cherry-pick students.

The objections are consistent and pervasive, so many school leaders and teachers subsequently avoid implementing the positive practices of these exemplary schools. Therefore, part I makes the important case for when readers should trust the research. Chapter 1 presents a typology of evidence, proceeding from level 1 research (personal beliefs) through level 5 research (preponderance of the evidence—the gold standard of educational research to which these chapters aspire). Chapter 2 then considers seven common challenges to educational research and offers a respectful reply to each challenge.

CHAPTER 1

Understand the Five Levels of Educational Research

Educators and leaders are weary of the vague claims that "research shows . . ." In conversations around the globe, they tell me that ambiguous claims are not enough to change their practices. They want to see credible evidence of the impact of improved leadership and teaching practices, and will not settle for claims without credible evidence. This chapter will help you to be a more critical consumer of educational research. Just as we ask students to evaluate claims based on the evidence, we must model that same level of critical thinking every time we listen to a presentation or read an article or book. As this chapter argues, there is an enormous difference between the credibility of a "journey story" about one person's experience—a sample size of one—and the highest level of research, the preponderance of evidence.

In this chapter, we explore five levels of educational research. These include (1) personal beliefs, (2) personal experiences, (3) collective experience, (4) systematic comparisons, and (5) preponderance of the evidence. When legislators and other policymakers, leaders, or teachers state, "Research shows that . . .," they might be referring to any one of these types of research. However, as citizens hoping to implement effective change in our schools, we can only truly rely on the higher levels of research—systematic comparison and preponderance of the evidence—to produce results that could feasibly be applicable and transferrable to our own schools. It is, therefore, essential that when we hear claims about research, we identify which type of research the people making the claims are using as the basis for their conclusions.

Level 1: Personal Beliefs

People are entitled to their own beliefs. That's a guarantee in the United States (thanks to the First Amendment to the Constitution), as well as in many other nations around the world. The United States is hardly unique in protecting freedom of beliefs. Indeed, the founding documents of the United States drew heavily from thought leaders in England, France, and many other countries (Lepore, 2018) where laws prohibit governments from interfering with the free exercise of anyone's religious beliefs, right to free speech, and freedom of assembly. As long as our beliefs do not interfere with the rights of others, we are free to believe whatever we wish.

Hand-in-hand with this freedom of personal beliefs, however, is the ability to believe something that is categorically wrong—and to persist in that belief due to personal preference, even in the face of evidence to the contrary. When presented with scientific evidence that defies personal beliefs, it is not unusual for someone to respond, proudly, "Your research may say that out-of-school suspension, punishment for missing homework, corporal punishment for behavioral infractions, and forcing students to stand in the corner with a dunce cap doesn't work, but it sure worked for me!" These claims are contrary to research and common sense (Reeves, 2011a), but in a free society, we tolerate them—at least as long as the actions associated with these claims do not harm others.

Whether the forum is a meeting of teachers, a public comment portion of a school board meeting, a legislative hearing, or a speech at a political rally, listeners must ask, "What type of research is this?" When the answer is a personal belief, unburdened by factual evidence, then we can accept it as a by-product of the constitutional guarantee of free speech and exclude it from the realm of evidence-based claims, no matter how sincerely held the belief may be. We cannot debate beliefs any more than we can debate sincerely held religious views. Rather, when encountering strongly held personal beliefs not based on evidence, one should respond respectfully, "Thank you for sharing your views. I want to assure you that I respect your beliefs and your right to hold them. I hope that you'll also respect other beliefs that are different from your own. Please don't confuse personal beliefs with evidence."

Level 2: Personal Experiences

The first level, personal beliefs, is based on sincerely held views that are sometimes supported by examples. Some teachers, administrators, and parents—and indeed some students—believe that grading as punishment is effective, even though a century of evidence undermines the veracity of that belief. The second level, personal experience, extends beyond belief statements and relies instead on what many educators regard as the most compelling evidence of all—their individual encounters with students. Beliefs do not spring from a void; they are often based on one's own learning and experiences. Many people who did well in school attend college and become educators or administrators. They formulate their beliefs about grading and discipline policies based on a system that is clearly effective for them. "It worked for me!" the opponents of grading and discipline reform will say. They are, of course, correct. Grading systems practices that are, according to the evidence, damaging (such as grading as punishment, the use of zeros on the hundred-point scale, and the use of the average; Reeves, 2011a) do, in fact, motivate some students to higher levels of performance. In my conversations with educators and administrators, I have asked, "For whom were these grading practices effective?" The most frequent answers are, "It worked for me!" and "It worked for my own children!" This is not surprising, coming from the viewpoint of college-educated professionals who are now public school educators. They loved school. They were good at school. They figured out the grading and discipline systems and responded well to rewards and punishments based on grades. The question is, What percentage of today's students do we expect to become public school educators? If the answer is less than 100 percent, then perhaps we should reconsider attributing to all students the same motivational scheme—grades as rewards and punishments—that were effective for many teachers. Personal anecdotal evidence may be powerful when forming our belief systems, but we must be careful about generalizing our personal experiences to all students. It is preferable to adopt an attitude of "There is always something to learn," and, indeed, I have seen teachers who, even in the final months of their careers, continue to improve their practices, learn from research, and change their techniques in order to better serve the cause of student learning.

Level 3: Collective Experience

Irving L. Janis (1982) coined the term *groupthink* to describe the tendency of people to acquiesce to the group and submerge their own better judgment. Sometimes the consequences are trivial, such as in psychological experiments in which subjects are shown two lines, clearly of different lengths, but other observers (confederates of the researchers) claim the lines are of equal length. If there is only one other person in the room, the research subjects hold their own, maintaining the lines are clearly different lengths. But as more people in the room claim the lines are of equal length, the research subjects cave to the inaccurate observations of the group (Heath & Heath, 2013). The consequences are less benign when the conversation participants are debating issues of greater importance.

Although an individual teacher may seek to change his or her practice—perhaps by calling on students randomly or by simply rearranging desks—professional isolation can be terribly lonely. Group experience provides the illusion of certainty, of unanimity, of proof: "It's not just me who believes this—it's the entire mathematics department! It's the entire third-grade team! Our faculty voted, and we are unanimous." Thus, popularity supplants reason. It is critical to remember, however, that even multiple instances of personal experiences or beliefs are still just personal experiences or beliefs. They remain anecdotal, and as such, are fallible in the absence of more credible research.

Level 4: Systematic Comparisons

Systematic comparisons produce some of the most effective and persuasive research that can directly influence professional practices. Consider the example of a teacher who makes an alteration to her teaching practice in the second semester. She can subsequently make three comparisons to form a very strong basis for research conclusions. The first is a comparison of the same group of students before and after the intervention. For example, the teacher can compare student performance in the first semester, when there was no change in professional practices, with student performance in the second semester, when the teacher altered a particular aspect of her practice. Perhaps it was a change in when students do homework—from at-home practice to in-school practice. Perhaps it was a change in the way the students revise and respond to teacher feedback. Perhaps it was the use of student self-assessment before submitting work to the teacher. The beauty of a systematic comparison is all other variables are held constant; the only change is the change in teacher professional practices. The students are the same, as are the schedule, curriculum, assessment, and teacher. If there is a change in results, it is very likely due to the change in teacher practice. In the second case, the teacher might make year-to-year comparisons, comparing the attendance, behavior, or academic performance in the first semester of one year to the first semester of the previous year. In these situations, the students are different, but the curriculum, assessments, time allocation, schedule, and teacher are the same. Finally, in the third case, the teacher might compare her results with the results of colleagues with similar students who did not change professional practices. Such studies allow for minimal variables and, hence, enable the teacher to draw powerful, generalizable conclusions about the effects of the professional practice she changed.

Every school and system, no matter how small or large, can conduct systematic comparisons like these. Teachers do not require a federal research grant, university evaluators, or any special expertise. *Reframing Teacher Leadership to Improve Your School* (Reeves, 2008b) provides a number of systematic comparisons examples at the elementary, middle, and high school levels.

Level 5: Preponderance of the Evidence

The apex of the research-type levels is when different researchers, operating independently using different research methods and working with subjects in different parts of the world, come to strikingly similar conclusions. For example, professionl learning facilitator Jenni Donohoo's (2017) synthesis of research finds that teacher efficacy is strongly related to gains in student achievement. John Hattie and colleagues also cite collective teacher efficacy as a powerful variable related to student results (Waack, n.d.). My own quantitative analysis of more than two thousand U.S. and Canadian schools places teacher efficacy at the top of the influences of student achievement over the course of three years (Reeves, 2011b). Qualitative researchers who engage in deep observations and case studies have come to remarkably similar conclusions (Hargreaves & Fullan, 2012). When focusing on level 5 research, we move away from the claims of dueling experts. Some of the reasons teachers may be cynical about education research are because "You can always find an expert to say anything," and "Today's claim may be discredited tomorrow," so they don't know what to believe. But if several different researchers using different methods in different places substantiate a claim, we are no longer looking at anecdotes or isolated claims, but rather at the *preponderance of the evidence.* Such research provides compelling evidence for why educators should try implementing a particular change in their schools.

The original 90/90/90 research was a hybrid of what this chapter describes as Level 3: Collective Experience and Level 4: Systematic Comparisons research. But in the second decade of the 21st century, the research on success in high-poverty schools is firmly rooted in Level 5: Preponderance of the Evidence. Different researchers using different methods operating independently have come to very similar conclusions about the elements of success in these schools and, most importantly, the replicability of those findings.

Summary

Advocates of improved teaching and leadership practices are caught in a quandary. When they propound good ideas without evidence, they are guilty of vacuous rhetoric. But even when they have evidence from a variety of sources and methods, they meet the wall of opposition labeled, "But it doesn't apply to me." The same argument could perhaps be made against any variety of medical interventions, as the research on pharmaceutical and surgical interventions is all performed on someone aside from the patient for whom those interventions are now recommended. In these cases, patients are wise to discount the experience of a single other patient, but they can often be persuaded based upon a combination of systematic comparisons—patients who survived compared to those who did not—and the preponderance of the evidence. While all research is imperfect, the application of the standards of evidence suggested in this chapter can offer the reader a thoughtful method for separating the most credible research from the rest.

CHAPTER 2

Decide Which Research to Trust

This chapter considers seven common challenges to educational research and offers a respectful reply to each challenge. Specifically, it considers seven arguments for research about success in high-poverty schools and how you might decide whether this research is worthy of your trust. The chapter concludes with a recommendation for locally generated research for the greatest level of credibility with teachers, administrators, and community members.

In the descriptions of the following seven arguments, I rely on extensive conversations with tens of thousands of teachers in fifty states and more than thirty countries. Whether the venue is Topeka or Tasmania, Louisiana or Lusaka, the arguments about research are strikingly consistent.

Argument 1: "The Research Doesn't Apply to Us"

When the locations of the research are anonymous, it lacks credibility with many teachers and administrators because of the deep suspicion that the participants in the studies are vastly different from the practitioners in their schools. The situation is similar to much of the psychological research performed not on the general population, but on college sophomores taking a psychology class (the students fill out surveys or participate in experiments week after week, all in the pursuit of their professor's publication). This is also one of many reasons so much psychological research is not replicable (Diener & Biswas-Diener, 2019). Similarly, if finding exceptional student performance results in the laboratory schools of universities and colleges, where students are often the children of exceptionally bright and committed graduate students and are only temporarily living on a low income, those results can hardly be labeled representative of the larger population of students from low-income families.

In the original equity and excellence research (Reeves, 2004), by contrast, every school was from public educational systems in the United States, and schools ranged in location from the West Coast (where there were also very high populations of students not speaking English at home), to the Midwest (where there was multigenerational poverty), to the eastern United States (where political upheaval, financial disasters, unemployment, and persistent social ills made for a difficult learning environment for students and a challenging working environment for teachers). None of the schools are exceptional, and none are university lab schools. Indeed, one of the most important elements when selecting schools for the study was they must be similar in every respect to the other unselected schools in the same system—the same union contract, per-pupil funding, teacher assignment policy, and neighborhoods. In other words, equity and excellence schools truly are representative of high-poverty schools across North America. The only differences are in academic achievement and the professional practices teachers and leaders employ to achieve those high levels of performance. It is also important to note that the programs in use did not distinguish the successful schools, but rather the differences were due to the specific actions of teachers and leaders. A consistent theme in the research is that practices, not programs, make the difference for student results.

It is important to regard equity and excellence research as the starting gate, not the finish line. Part II (page 29) of this book addresses *what* equity and excellence schools do differently, and part III (page 89) describes *how* they do it, but equally important is the information in part IV (page 137), which requires the continual assessing of implementation through accountability systems. In order to institutionalize the most effective practices for your school or district, it is imperative for you to create a continuous cycle of professional learning that links the *causes* of academic achievement with the *effects*. Only in this way will you know, based on data from *your* students in *your* school and community, the professional practices most effective for you. I believe equity and excellence research makes an effective case that the practices in the following chapters are strongly associated with improved student achievement. However, I readily acknowledge that the most effective way to sustain effective practice is not merely by reading the research of others but also by committing to local observation and research to overcome the objection, "We are different."

Despite efforts to match equity and excellence schools in other low-income schools across North America, it is certainly true that no external sample of schools will precisely mirror the characteristics of the school or district in which you work. Every sample, whether from a few schools the researcher chooses as a sample of convenience or a larger sample that closely mirrors the characteristics of students in the original research, is limited because practitioners contend, "That sample did not include my students and my school." Indeed, even when the sample does address this challenge by including "my students in my schools," skeptics could contend the sample used last year's students and this year's students are different.

The only response to this challenge is not to argue over the representative nature of samples, but to shift the research focus from external to internal. In *Reframing Teacher Leadership to Improve Your School* (Reeves, 2008b), I offer a method for teachers to conduct and assess action research that has, in my experience, been transformative for promoting effective and sustainable change. This method is colloquially referred to as the *science fair approach,* as the method mirrors the three-panel cardboard displays fourth graders often use for their science fair projects. Although the research topics vary widely based on the individual needs of each teacher and school, the format of these three-panel cardboard displays is consistent.

1. **Left panel:** Challenge

2. **Middle panel:** Professional practices

3. **Right panel:** Results

Here are some examples from schools I observed.

- **Challenge:** High school failures due to missing work (more than 90 percent of D and F grades were due to missing work, not attendance or behavior).

- **Professional practices:** Teachers implemented a daily required intervention immediately before lunch. All students used the same agenda, and all teachers agreed to use a stamp system to indicate when students completed the work. When students were missing a stamp, they were directed to the appropriate room to complete the work.

- **Results:** D and F grades declined by 67 percent in one semester.

- **Challenge:** Middle school behavior was out of control and suspensions at an all-time high.
- **Professional practices:** Teachers implemented restorative justice schoolwide and agreed on a chart of responses for what is required for in-class, in-office, and out-of-school discipline.
- **Results:** Suspensions decreased by 55 percent in one year.

- **Challenge:** Chronic absenteeism in elementary through high school.
- **Professional practices:** Teachers implemented the sixty-second report— all students not seated in the classroom within one minute of the tardy bell were added to a list in the principal's office and called within the first twenty minutes of school. All staff members who were not in front of students attended a stand-up meeting in the principal's office.
- **Results:** Absenteeism decreased by more than 80 percent in one year.

- **Challenge:** Excessive middle and high school failures due to missing work and student disengagement. Students who accumulated zeros on the one-hundred-point scale quit trying because they knew no matter how hard they worked, they would fail the class.
- **Professional practices:** Teachers changed from the one-hundred-point scale to a simple A–F grading system, where A = 4, B = 3, C = 2, D = 1, and F = 0. Teachers also switched from calculating the final semester grade based on the average of all work to giving a final grade based on the teacher's judgment of student proficiency from the latest and best evidence of student learning.
- **Results:** D and F grades decreased 38 percent in social studies, 45 percent in English, and 62 percent in mathematics.

The consistent element of the science fair approach is that it uses local research with local students in local schools—*your* students in *your* school or district. Instead of considering a different sample of students from a different school, no matter how representative, the science fair approach allows teachers to compare the same students from the same neighborhoods with the same demographics with the same teachers within the same year. This compelling before-and-after approach allows teachers to conclude that all the other factors influencing student achievement are consistent— the only change is the teachers' changes in professional practices.

Argument 2: "Anecdotes Are Not Evidence"

The assertion, "Anecdotes do not equal evidence," is a very fair criticism, as many articles and books in education are best described as *journey stories*—the experience of a single teacher or administrator. However informative these experiences may be, they are anecdotes, not research. This is why we must all be critical consumers of educational research when a speaker or writer blithely claims, "Studies show . . . " or "Research says . . . ," when the studies or research may only be a sample size of one. This does not eliminate the value of case studies, but it is much more helpful to draw inferences when researchers accumulate a large number of cases. Certain educational researchers are leading the way in studying the successful practices of multiple school districts and condensing the results into a format educational leaders and teachers can implement in their schools. For example, Heather Zavadsky (2009), director of research and implementation at the Texas High School Project, analyzes the workings of several well-run school districts in her book *Bringing School Reform to Scale: Five Award-Winning Urban Districts*. Reflection on a single high-performing urban system is not nearly as helpful as Zavadsky's (2009) synthesis of a variety of school systems and her ability to find common elements despite differences in geography, governance systems, funding, and student populations.

Using the science fair approach discussed previously, teachers may think their own work is "just an anecdote" and therefore not worthy of being shared with colleagues. But when that individual experience is grouped with dozens or hundreds of colleagues' experiences, then patterns can emerge that no longer rely on anecdotal evidence. Moreover, a focus on teaching practices allows educators to distinguish between *programs* and *practices*. Vendors would like to claim a particular program, curriculum, or technology application leads to gains in student achievement, but programs alone accomplish nothing. The overwhelming conclusion of our review of more than two thousand school plans (Reeves, 2011a) is that it is practices, not programs, that hold the key for improvement in student results. In addition, a focus on practices turns the analytical lens where it belongs—on practices that are replicable rather than the mystical qualities of the individual teacher. Kim Marshall (personal communication, September 16, 2019), educational researcher and author of *The Marshall Memo* website (https://marshallmemo.com), thoughtfully distinguishes between *teachers* and *teaching* by noting that when the focus is on the teacher, great practice is relegated to the ethereal realm ("She's just a gifted teacher!") or calumny ("He's just a terrible teacher!"). Neither of those observations is particularly insightful guidance for any professional beyond the superficial "Be good and don't be bad." But, as Marshall suggests, when we focus on teaching—the actual practices in which teachers engage—then we can address specific practices in discipline, feedback, curriculum, lesson planning, and professional responsibilities to perform effectively. The guidance is not, "Be more like Ms. Smith," but rather like the following.

- "It's important that you move around and are close to the students, not remain behind your desk."

- "It's important that you give students immediate feedback during class, not just on their papers several days after they did the work."

- "It's important that you engage every student by using whiteboards, cold calling, or similar techniques, and not merely recognize students who raise their hands."

These concrete practices focus on what teachers actually do, not who they are as people. Moreover, these are practices coaches and administrators can model in real time, showing their colleagues in the classroom that no matter one's responsibility in the school, they are all teachers and must be willing to show they still have the ability to demonstrate to colleagues and students the importance of effective teaching practices.

Argument 3: "The Research Depends on Heroic Teachers and Administrators Whose Efforts Are Unsustainable"

Movies about high-poverty-turned-high-performance schools often feature a particularly resourceful, motivated, or heroic teacher who enters the classroom and leaves masterful change in his or her wake. Moviegoers see this in films like *Stand and Deliver* (Musca & Menéndez, 1988) or *Freedom Writers* (DeVito, Shamberg, Sher, & LaGravenese, 2007). Although the storylines are compelling, the teachers in these moving tales do not represent the average teachers who, thrust into a high-poverty school often with inadequate preparation and support, are fighting to maintain a modicum of discipline, stay one page ahead of the students in the curriculum, and learn the craft of teaching.

I acknowledge there are exceptional teachers in successful high-poverty schools, but the equity and excellence research deliberately avoids these out-of-the-ordinary cases. The schools we learn the most from have the same teacher assignment policy, same union contract, same per-pupil funding, and in many cases, same school and classroom architecture as their less-successful counterparts. Great teachers make for compelling stories, but greater *teaching* is the only credible source of replicable and sustainable practice.

Argument 4: "Publishers' Research Is Commercially Tainted"

The history of commercially tainted research in education is a long one. Just as purveyors of sugar- and processed-food-funded research purport to show their products are healthy—research that led to a multigenerational increase in obesity—so also do the sellers of video games attempt to show these are indispensable tools for student learning (Egenfeldt-Nielsen, 2006). This challenge is certainly not limited to the field of education. Although one would think that medical research is at the apex of credibility, the fact is, commercially funded research is more likely to be published than studies of higher quality and free of commercial bias (Hogan, Sellar, & Lingard, 2015; Lynch et al., 2007).

There is a significant burden on school administrators and other decision makers to be critical consumers. They must understand the nature of the research to influence purchasing decisions and the degree to which that research is applicable to the conditions of the schools and districts of the purchasers. One of the most frequently misunderstood terms is *significance,* which, in the context of research, almost always means *statistical significance.* In simple terms, the differences between two groups are considered statistically significant if an analysis of those differences shows they are unlikely (less than a 5 percent chance) to be different due to random variation. For example, if a group of students who participate in a particular instructional reading intervention score 79 percent on a test, and another group of students who did not participate in that reading intervention score 75 percent, then researchers can compare those two groups and, based on the number of students in the groups and the variation in their scores, determine that the difference between 79 percent and 75 percent is unlikely due to randomness. But that is a very different proposition than saying the reading program *caused* the students in the first group to score higher. Medical researchers sometimes use the term *clinical significance* to distinguish a finding so important it is worth changing one's practice. Although there are many treatments, pharmaceuticals, and practices associated with statistically significant differences, most of those changes are insufficient to lead doctors to prescribe a different drug or use a different treatment modality (Leyva De Los Rios, 2017). This is because for every treatment a physician begins, there is usually another treatment that must be withdrawn. Similarly, starting a new reading program usually means withdrawing an old reading program. Therefore, the decision maker must consider not only the impact of adding a new program but also the impact of withdrawing the old program.

The failure to distinguish the importance of *clinical significance* compared to *statistical significance* was first illustrated during the Race to the Top era (2009–2017), during which federal grant incentives led districts to pile one program on top of another. Each program might have been significant when compared with no program, but almost none showed value when they were simply part of a constellation of many duplicative programs. I observed schools with three different data-analysis protocols, two different mathematics programs, and seven different literacy programs, which all vied for the time and attention of teachers who, not surprisingly, were unable to implement any of these new and expensive programs well. There were no grants for educational leaders who decided to stop doing something. My research (Reeves, 2011b), based on more than two thousand school plans, demonstrates that when schools have more than six instructional initiatives, student performance declines, even as those schools spend more money and acquire more programs. Moreover, the most fragmented schools—those burdened by more and more programs—are most likely to be schools with high percentages of students from low-income families, high percentages of students who are learning English, and high percentages of students with special needs (Reeves, 2011b). In brief, the schools most needing focused leadership are the least likely to have it. It is no wonder the programs claiming "significance" in the laboratory or another controlled setting did not exhibit similar results in the real world of teachers and students overwhelmed by multiple demands on their time from many different programs.

To be clear, I am not suggesting that the differences between the research claims of the advocates of educational programs and the reality teachers and administrators experience are due to malice or corruption on the part of vendors. Rather, I am making the observation that the environment the research salespeople cite may be substantially different from the environment of the practitioners who actually try to use these programs in the real world. Therefore, it is essential for people making buying decisions to inquire about the actual environment of the research. Moreover, major decisions about curriculum, assessment, instructional practices, leadership techniques, and financial commitments are always better informed if leaders follow the discipline of mutually exclusive decision making (Lafley, Martin, Rivkin, & Siggelkow, 2012). Good leaders can make bad decisions if they fail to practice the fundamental disciplines of gathering information and considering alternative hypotheses (Campbell, Whitehead, & Finkelstein, 2009).

In order to be more critical consumers of research, leaders must persistently ask, "If I am going to decide to implement *X*, then what will I give up—in time, money, and professional energy?" One of the great traps in this line of inquiry is the myth that because a grant funds a new initiative, it is therefore free. But no decision is free. Even if there is no impact on the budget, there is definitely an impact on time and attention. Because leaders cannot monitor and focus on more than about half a dozen major initiatives, every additional initiative beyond that threshold, even if it appears to be cost-free, not only takes a toll on the leader's time and attention but also encroaches on every other initiative in the system.

The only remedy for this is organizational and leadership focus. Effective strategic plans are not merely an accumulation of programs and tasks to be implemented. Rather, strategy is also the art of deciding what not to do. My experience suggests that the primary complaint that teachers have is *time*. They are intelligent and hard-working, but simply overwhelmed with the sheer quantity of tasks they are expected to accomplish. Therefore, leaders recognize that time is a zero-sum game—every hour allocated to one task is an hour not available for another. The focused leader who, for example, wants to encourage collaborative scoring of student work in order to deliver consistent expectations of students and reliable scoring by teachers provides time in staff meetings and collaborative team meetings to accomplish those important tasks. That means that the focused leader is deciding not only that collaborative scoring is vital but also that competing activities in those meetings—like the primitive practice of making verbal announcements—will be discarded. While many leaders claim to value focus, few can articulate how they will save time by discontinuing announcements, stop the expectations that texts and emails be responded to within minutes of receipt, and ban classroom activities—such as twenty-year-old word search puzzles—that have zero educational value. When leaders decide what to stop doing, teachers know that they and their time are respected.

Argument 5: "Results Are Distorted Because the Criteria for Success Are Too Low"

Many studies of high-poverty schools' success sometimes receive criticism because readers claim the schools' standards for success are too low and not reflective of success in the real world. For example, the New York Regents exam provides a four-point scale for students, and a score of three or four is regarded as passing (Pondiscio, 2019). It could be argued that the bar should be higher, but the plain fact is that only a minority of urban schools in New York meet the standard of a three. In the original equity and excellence research (Reeves, 2004), the criterion for meeting standards is only at the *basic* level, which was the criteria at that time used by the state. Some critics have approached me in meetings and argued that this bar is too low to count as success. But in that review of 135 high-poverty schools, only seven met the basic criteria. Few people argue against setting the bar high for student achievement with classroom expectations to match, but when only seven of 135 schools meet a criterion, it seemed to me that it was, to put it mildly, evidence of comparative success. Thus, these U.S. schools met the state criteria at a far higher level than most schools with similar demographic characteristics. But the criticism is nevertheless well taken. In many states, students can score only 40 percent of the answers on the test correctly and still be labeled proficient. Part of the flaw in descriptions of *proficient* is that proficiency is a moving target. Even in states claiming a commitment to standards-based education for more than two decades, some change the *cut scores*—the percentage of correct answers the state deems adequate—every year. If too few students and schools do well, then the state lowers the cut score. If too many of the students and schools do well, then the state raises the cut score. This procedure is precisely the opposite of standards-based assessment. Safety professionals do not, for example, relax or strengthen the criteria for left-hand turns for teenage drivers or safe landings for pilots based on annual variations in other drivers' or pilots' performance. The standard is the standard. This is also a reason the best and most reliable measurements of student achievement are based on consistent criteria during the same year in a class with largely the same students, teacher, curriculum, and assessments. Although this emphasis on consistency is imperfect, it is far superior to attempts to draw inferences about student success when the tests and criteria for proficiency change from one year to the next, and when the students compared are also different from one year to the next.

In the absence of a national assessment of student performance, accompanied by a systematic analysis of teaching and leadership practices in every school, the best data that we have is that provided by districts and states. This leads to inevitable variation about what *success* really means. While that is a legitimate concern, it does not deny the fact that when the same assessment is given to a wide variety of students in the same subject and same grade with the same socioeconomic status, some do better than others. The explanation is neither money nor zip code, but teaching and leadership practices. The United States does provide the National Assessment of Educational Progress (NAEP), labeled the "Nation's Report Card," but it offers nothing in the way of school-by-school analysis of instructional and leadership practices.

Argument 6: "The Funding Is Higher for Successful Schools"

It is true that successful high-poverty schools often have higher levels of funding than other schools without high populations of students from low-income families. This is almost always due to their eligibility for Title I funds, which the U.S. Department of Education allocates to all high-poverty schools. One goal of equity and excellence research was to ensure the findings would transfer to all schools, so our methodology included carefully monitoring the levels of per-pupil funding. By doing this, the successful and unsuccessful schools under review had nearly identical per-pupil funding. As a result, readers can implement the findings with confidence that the differences in success are, in fact, due to changes in teaching practices and not due to a particularly high level of funding.

Because federal Title I funds are distributed on the basis of the percentage of students eligible for free or reduced-price lunch, it is not unusual to find high-poverty schools and districts with higher levels of per-pupil funding than schools which are not eligible for Title I funds because they serve a more affluent population. On the other hand, more affluent schools benefit from a higher residential property tax base, and therefore enjoy economic advantages. But whatever the source and rationale for funding, the consistent findings of the research cited earlier in this book is that while money is important for schools, money alone is not the variable that determines student success. High-poverty schools benefit not only from Title I funds but also from a plethora of grants and special allocations designed to support one initiative after another. This funding creates the illusion of prosperity because these schools are flooded with people and programs all designed with good intentions. But the reality is the schools are fragmented in so many different directions that administrators cannot monitor effective implementation of the programs, and the teachers do not have time to focus on any single program in order to provide effective implementation. The key to success is not funding; it is in the specific implementation of carefully selected teaching practices.

Argument 7: "Successful Schools Cherry-Pick Students"

An argument frequently levelled against magnet and charter schools is that some, but by no means all, have higher levels of success because they can select, or cherry-pick, their students. Yes, the critics argue, a high percentage of students might be from low-income families (Bambrick-Santoyo, 2018; Pondiscio, 2019). But if the school has a low percentage of special education students or students with significant discipline problems, mental health issues, or learning disabilities, then it cannot be compared to schools with similar student demographics that have significantly greater percentages of students with these same needs. This is a very fair concern, and it is a reason reviewers of successful high-poverty schools case studies should ask questions about the extent of the special education population—Is it similar to or different from the schools it is being compared to? Even if the allocation of students with special needs is identical, however, there is no question that students in magnet and charter schools have parents who made the effort to enter a lottery or otherwise advocate for their children to attend a particular school. As Pondiscio (2019) acknowledges, successful charter schools may not cherry-pick students, but they certainly cherry-pick parents, as the lottery systems on which most of them depend require parents to submit applications, take an interest in their children, and in some cases, make extra efforts to ensure on-time attendance and help students adhere to strict discipline and academic policies that are not always present in traditional public schools. That is almost never the case for children in homeless shelters, living with adults who are not their parents or who otherwise do not take an interest in education. These children are generally left to their own devices for entry into selective schools. The same concern is true for exam schools, where (in Boston and New York, for example) the score on a single exam decides who will be admitted to Boston Latin School or The Bronx High School of Science and who will not (Gay, 2019a; New York Times Editorial Board, 2019). Although the demographics may be similar to non-exam schools, there is no question that if a school starts with the top 1 percent of students in exam-taking ability, that school will show higher degrees of success when the measurement is, most commonly, exam-taking ability.

Of all the criticisms of the research on successful high-poverty schools, the issue of cherry-picking is of the gravest concern, particularly for successful charter schools. While lotteries generally ensure that these schools have comparable percentages of special education students to traditional public school, the challenge of cherry-picked parents is real and legitimate, as even the staunchest defenders of charter schools acknowledge (Pondiscio, 2019). But there are three essential responses to this challenge that teachers and leaders in any school, regardless of label or governance structure, must consider. First, the evidence on successful high-poverty schools is certainly not limited to charter schools or others that are otherwise selective. The more than a dozen sources cited in the introduction (page 1) and chapter 1 (page 9) provide many examples of success far beyond charter schools. Second, and more to the point, so what if successful schools engage parents more directly and benefit from discipline and academic policies that parents wholeheartedly endorse? That is not an argument that these schools are failing or that their policies are inadequate, but rather that all schools—traditional public, charter, and private—can learn from the teaching and leadership practices of their counterparts. Third, and most importantly, the most successful charter schools, such as New York's Success Academy, can be compared to schools that actually do cherry-pick students—that is, the designated gifted and talented schools. Under this sort of comparison, the students selected by lottery in the Success Academy Charter Schools significantly outperform the highly selected—cherry-picked, if you will—gifted and talented schools (Pondiscio, 2019).

Summary

This chapter considered seven criticisms of research about success in high-poverty schools. To be clear, I do not challenge the motives of critics, as I fundamentally believe that almost everyone who enters into the national and global discussion about how to improve education has the best interests of students at heart. Nevertheless, this book has a clear point of view, and I want to respectfully acknowledge and respond to the most common criticisms of the research on successful high poverty schools. Critics frequently contend that successful high-poverty schools are different—whether due to their funding, students, or exceptional teachers—and therefore, their results cannot be generalized to conditions in unsuccessful schools. Many of the articles, books, and films about successful high-poverty schools are no more than anecdotes consisting of a sample size of one, and not generalizable. Some research, particularly regarding commercial programs, curricula, and technology, may be commercially tainted if the organization sells and administers those programs. Some successful high-poverty schools are based on criteria that are too low; we ought to expect more from all students. The funding for some successful high-poverty schools may be higher than the funding for unsuccessful schools. Finally, successful high-poverty schools, particularly magnet and charter schools, may cherry-pick their students, either by excluding high-needs students or by relying on parents who take an active interest in their children's education, factors that are not always the case in the unsuccessful high-poverty schools.

The best response to these criticisms is to acknowledge and respect them, be aware of them when conducting research and presenting findings, and do the best job possible to take these potential criticisms into account when conducting future research. Most important, good researchers acknowledge the limitations of their work, as I have sought to do in this chapter. That said, acknowledgment of potential limitations does not invalidate the research findings. This book describes not a single student or case, but rather the preponderance of evidence from a variety of scholars. This is the apex of research quality readers can rely on when making decisions about which teaching practices to implement in their own schools.

Prepared with an excellent understanding of educational research and when it can (or cannot) be trusted, you are ready to delve into the fruits of research on successful high-poverty schools—the teaching practices that high-performing, high-poverty schools use differently. The following section will discuss seven teaching practices of equity and excellence schools you can use and implement in your own schools and classrooms starting right now.

PART II

Understanding What Equity and Excellence Schools Do Differently

After visiting all the equity and excellence schools, my colleagues and I noticed profound differences between the assessment and instructional practices of these schools and those of low-achieving schools (Reeves, 2004). This section presents seven different teaching practices equity and excellence schools incorporate to improve student achievement. This is not a recipe for success, or a cookie-cutter set of programs. Rather, the following chapters describe the specific practices that distinguish successful high-poverty schools from their well-intentioned but less successful counterparts.

These findings have been surprisingly robust over time, clearly separating transient fads and programs from practices that have enduring value. Of the seven practices described in these chapters, only the focus on professional learning communities is new. While the original research considered the value of collaboration, the latest and best evidence on learning communities suggests the value of a more intentional structure for effective collaboration (see a wide variety of specific examples of the impact of the Professional Learning Communities at Work® process at the non-commercial website, AllThingsPLC.info). It is no accident that the number of these suggestions is small. In contrast to school improvement plans I have seen with scores of priorities—I've reviewed school plans with more than seventy priorities and district plans with more than two hundred priorities and programs—these seven key ideas correspond to the value of focus that my large-scale quantitative study suggested (Reeves, 2011a). Moreover, this emphasis on focus is consistent with recent global observations from author, speaker, and educational consultant Michael Fullan (2016).

Chapters 3 through 9 each discuss one of the following recommended practices.

1. Organize their school or district as a professional learning community.

2. Display a laser-like focus on student achievement.

3. Conduct collaborative scoring.

4. Emphasize nonfiction writing.

5. Utilize frequent formative assessment with multiple opportunities for success.

6. Perform constructive data analysis.

7. Engage in cross-disciplinary units of instruction.

Each chapter includes specific observations useful for readers seeking to translate theory into practice.

CHAPTER 3

Organize Their School or District as a Professional Learning Community

When I first observed equity and excellence schools, I noticed they were built around collaborative teams of teachers, coaches, and administrators. In the intervening years, thanks to the work of Richard DuFour, Robert Eaker, Rebecca DuFour, Tom Many, Mike Mattos, and others who have followed in their footsteps, we have a vocabulary for this sort of collaboration—*professional learning communities* (PLC; DuFour, DuFour, Eaker, Many, & Mattos, 2016). This is the central organizing principle of successful schools, whatever their demographics. Thus, in this first chapter on what equity and excellence schools do differently, we will discuss the key principles involved in organizing a school as a PLC.

In this chapter, we will establish the essential components of a PLC and identify how schools can become a PLC in both name *and* actions. We will conclude by discussing how leaders can keep focus within the PLC to maximize the advantages of collaboration.

Establishing the Essential Components of a PLC

When legendary football coach Vince Lombardi of the Green Bay Packers would begin practice each year, he would hold the pigskin above his head and say to his grizzled professional athletes, "Gentlemen, this is a football" (Bleier, 2019). It is in that spirit that even schools engaged in the work of PLCs for decades must continuously renew their commitment to the essentials of the process.

The late Richard DuFour, the foremost proponent of PLCs along with Robert Eaker, once admonished me for my imprecision in language relating to PLCs. Like many educators, I referred to "PLC time" and "PLC meetings." But he reminded me, "Professional learning communities represent the organizing principle for the entire school. It is who we are as a system, not the work of a single grade level or department" (R. DuFour, personal communication, October 31, 2015).

DuFour et al. (2016) are equally clear about the three big ideas that drive the work of PLCs.

1. A focus on learning. The first (and the biggest) of the big ideas is based on the premise that *the fundamental purpose of the school is to ensure that all students learn at high levels (grade level or higher)*. This focus on and commitment to the learning of each student are the very essence of a *learning* community. (DuFour et al., 2016, p. 11)

2. A collaborative culture and collective responsibility. The second big idea driving the PLC process is that in order to ensure all students learn at high levels, *educators must work collaboratively and take collective responsibility for the success of each student.* (DuFour et al., 2016, p. 11)

3. A results orientation. The third big idea that drives the work of PLCs is the need for a *results orientation*. To assess their effectiveness in helping all students learn, educators in a PLC focus on results—evidence of student learning. They then use that evidence of learning to inform and improve their professional practice and respond to individual students who need intervention or enrichment. (DuFour et al., 2016, p. 12)

PLCs have the following essential characteristics.

- Members of a PLC work together in collaborative teams rather than in isolation and take collective responsibility for student learning.

- Collaborative teams in a PLC establish a guaranteed and viable curriculum that specifies the knowledge, skills, and disciplines students are expected to acquire, unit by unit.

- Teams use an assessment process that includes frequent, team-developed, common formative assessments based on the guaranteed and viable curriculum.

- Teams use the results of common formative assessments to:

    a. Identify students who need additional time and support for learning

    b. Identify students who would benefit from enriched or extended learning

    c. Identify and address areas of individual strengths or weaknesses in teaching based on the evidence of student learning

    d. Identify and address areas where none of the team members were able to bring students to the desired level of proficiency

- PLCs create a system of interventions that guarantees struggling students receive additional time and support in ways that do not remove them from new direct instruction, regardless of the teacher to whom they are assigned.

Collaborative teams within PLCs focus on the following four critical questions (DuFour et al., 2016).

1. What do we want students to know and be able to do? (Learning)

2. How will we know if they learned it? (Assessment)

3. What will we do if they have not learned it? (Intervention)

4. What will we do if they already have learned it? (Extension)

While many schools devote most of their attention to curriculum, standards, and learning expectations (learning); less attention to common formative assessments; even less attention to specific student intervention plans; and least of all, the time devoted to extension of learning for students who need challenges far beyond their grade-level standards, the goal of PLCs should be to ensure high levels of learning for all students. Time should be given to each critical question; however, more time may be given to some of them.

Becoming a PLC in Name and Actions

In an analysis of data from more than 750,000 students, I found that schools engaged in the PLC process with depth and duration consistently display greater gains in student achievement, particularly in reading, mathematics, and science (Reeves, 2015). Further, schools implementing the PLC process for three, five, seven, or ten years perform at significantly higher levels than schools just beginning their PLC journey or schools with three years or fewer into that work. But this is the essence of the challenge because three, five, seven, and ten years is an eternity in schools. After three years, there may very well be a change in leadership, particularly in high-poverty schools (Levin & Bradley, 2019). Although a previous leader may have committed to organizing the school as a PLC, new leaders often fancy themselves as change agents and may not carry on the PLC implementation (or any initiative, however promising) with any real depth. This leaves too many schools functioning as ineffective PLCs, which DuFour and I call *PLC lite* (DuFour & Reeves, 2016).

PLC lite is an exercise in futility that helps neither students nor the educational systems that serve them. Too many schools have engaged in the illusion that their school is a PLC when, in fact, the staff have done little more than change the name of the staff meeting. Team members gather in the same room, but instead of facing one another, they sit in their own spaces and engage in private activities on their electronic devices. Topics such as announcements, field trips, and student discipline dominate these gatherings, and there is barely a hint of the four questions that focus on learning, assessment, intervention, and extension.

PLC lite schools are unlikely to enjoy the full benefits of collaborative teaching, irrespective of how many years they have been structured as a PLC. For educators and students alike, to display the achievement gains possible when functioning as a PLC, schools must strive to continuously improve by following the PLC principles consistently over a period of many years. These schools must take collective responsibility for student achievement, a guaranteed and viable curriculum, and a focus on the four questions. In sum, the mere label *PLC* is wholly unsatisfactory. Leaders must have a clear vision of what a PLC must be and do.

Keeping Focus in a PLC

Here's a provocative question to consider: Who has the authority to spend a million dollars in your school and district? Even in a very large system, million-dollar authority is usually at a fairly high level (board president, superintendent, and perhaps deputy superintendent). But the truth is—the newest administrative assistant in your system can schedule meetings that consume a million dollars or more (Mankins & Garton, 2017). Consider the modest assumption that teachers earn, on average, $40,000 per year. That's about thirty-two dollars per hour assuming a thirty-six-week school year and a seven-hour day. Multiply the thirty-two dollars by thirty teachers in a building and by thirty-six meetings per year, and you're over $34,000.

Educational leaders who aspire to focus their work on effective PLCs must therefore be clear about what they will not do. They will not, for example, divert previous hours away from collaborative team time that is at the heart of PLC implementation in order to have administrative meetings that are burdened by administrative announcements and passive acceptance by the educators who participate. They will not accept curriculum additions that are not within the scope of the foundational PLC response to question 1: What do we want students to know and be able to do? They will not accept assessments that are disconnected from the curriculum, even if those assessments bear seductive labels such as *formative* or *benchmark*. In the context of a PLC, assessments are only of value if they are clearly linked to the question of what we want students to know and be able to do. Otherwise, these assessments are not formative, but rather better labeled as *uninformative*. In order to be formative, an assessment must bridge the PLC discussion from the first two questions about learning and assessment to the third and fourth questions about intervention and extensions of learning. Focus, in sum, is not merely about deciding what to do. Rather, it requires vigilance in protecting the time of teachers and administrators so that they can focus on what matters most.

Summary

In this chapter, we considered the essential components of PLCs as well as the more common practices that elevate the label over the practice. In this case, we are left not with a PLC, but a *PLC lite*. We also considered research that strongly suggests PLC implementation takes time; the schools that implemented PLCs over three, five, seven, and ten years ago show remarkably greater gains in student achievement than schools with just a few years of implementation. Often, the schools most in need of support—those with high-poverty students—are least likely to have stable and consistent leadership. Schools must commit to the PLC process even through cases of leadership change, and leaders must have a clear vision of what a PLC must be and do.

Once a school or district is organized as a PLC, it can begin following the other practices found in equity and excellence schools. The next chapter will discuss the laser-like focus on student achievement that is key in all high-poverty, high-performing schools.

CHAPTER 4

Display a Laser-Like Focus on Student Achievement

Although I've never been in a school that does not claim to focus on student achievement, a quality distinguishes equity and excellence schools from other schools: they transform vague claims and aspirations into specific practices. First, and most important, equity and excellence schools have a laser-like focus on student achievement. This chapter reviews the specific and tangible ways equity and excellence schools demonstrate their focus on student achievement.

First, these schools display visible indicators—tangible and highly visible reminders on the school walls and in the trophy cases—that student achievement is the goal. Second, these schools allocate time differently, and they hold formal and informal conversations that vary dramatically from other schools. Third, their leadership is focused almost entirely on students and not on the many administrative demands that can consume the minutes, hours, and days of most school leaders. Fourth, their relationships with students and colleagues are remarkable for their intensity, depth, and personalization.

Considering What's on the Walls

One of the most prominent differences between high- and low-achieving schools comes down to a simple factor—What's on the walls? Even the most casual observer in an equity and excellence school cannot walk down a hallway without seeing charts, graphs, and tables displaying student achievement information, as well as data about continuous student improvement. The data are on display not only in principals' offices but also throughout the schools. In addition, school trophy cases full of exemplary academic work (such as clear, concise essays; wonderful science projects; terrific social studies papers; student art work; musical compositions; and outstanding mathematics papers) are abundant. In short, equity and excellence schools make it clear to all observers—including students—that outstanding academic performance is highly prized.

The strategic use of the trophy case is not limited to academic work. Certainly, there is a place for athletic trophies, as well as for awards from the many extracurricular and academic competitions in which students excel. However, equity and excellence schools take their displays one step further. Along with the trophies are examples of student artwork, musical compositions, original poetry and dramatic works, and additional real student work that led to the awards and trophies. One middle school dedicates a trophy case to student goals. It contains the written hopes and aspirations of more than eight hundred students, encased in glass and immune from graffiti. Every hallway in this school visibly shows that the school staff care not only about collectively earned trophies but also about the individual accomplishments of each student.

Making the Most of the Leader's Time

Every school in a district has a certain number of minutes in the day to allocate for classes, lunches, staff meetings, planning periods, and so on. But there is a difference in how equity and excellence schools allocate time. Their laser-like focus on student achievement is evident in the formal and informal conversations of grade-level, department, and entire-staff meetings. No time is wasted on announcements, but rather time is spent exclusively on discussions about teaching and learning. When I asked one equity and excellence principal, whose district had won the Broad Prize for being the best urban school district in the United States, how she finds time for all the work she and the faculty do on common assessments and data analysis plus their relentless focus on student achievement, she said, "I don't have more time than anybody else. I just stopped doing faculty meetings three years ago. We spend every moment we have on student achievement. And besides," she added, "making oral announcements to adults is primitive" (L. Capsen, personal communication, November 1, 1997).

While many schools allocate time for teacher collaboration under the banner of PLCs, the phenomenon of PLC lite (as discussed in the previous chapter) results in schools that have time allocated for collaboration but fritter it away without the laser-like focus on student achievement, the hallmark of effective PLCs. In equity and excellence schools, however, not a second of collaborative time is wasted, and every meeting has a purpose. Principals, administrators, and instructional coaches may not be in every meeting, but they monitor how the time is spent. Others use a very simple four-line email the collaborative teams complete in the final portion of every meeting. The four email lines correspond to the four critical question of a PLC (DuFour et al., 2016):

1. What do we want students to know and be able to do? (Learning)

2. How will we know if they have learned it? (Assessment)

3. What will we do if they don't learn it? (Intervention)

4. What will we do if they already have learned it? (Extension)

However, it's not always possible or even necessary for a collaborative team to address every question in every situation. For example, early in the year, there is often a heavy focus on the first question so all classes in the same grade and subject have a consistent curriculum. Additionally, because using common formative assessments is a key to an effectively functioning PLC, a school might devote extra time to the second question. But over the course of every month, principals can reasonably expect teachers to address all four questions. The ultimate goal is for schools to ensure high levels of learning for all and to avoid PLC lite by addressing all four questions every month. Schools can track progress by completing a simple four-bar frequency chart at the end of each month to show how the school as a whole addressed the four questions in collaborative team meetings. If all the teams addressed all four questions, those four bars should be equal, as can be seen in figure 4.1.

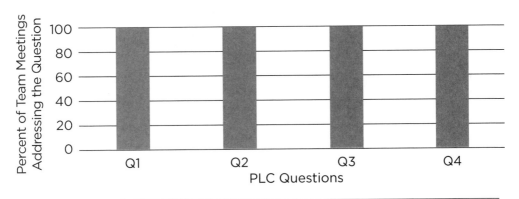

Figure 4.1: The hypothetical PLC profile.

However, my experience is that the actual time allocation tends to be uneven, with the most time allocated to lesson planning (learning), somewhat less time for common assessments, even less for intervention, and least of all for extension, as figure 4.2 suggests.

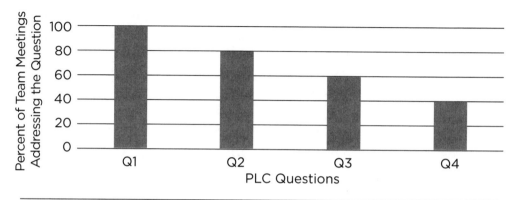

Figure 4.2: The common PLC profile.

These simple displays (see figure 4.1, page 39 and figure 4.2) allow faculty members to make frequent midcourse corrections in how they allocate collaborative team time. For example, after reviewing figure 4.2, faculty members might observe, "We've devoted so much time to lesson planning and intervention for low-performing students that we've failed to address the needs of students who are already proficient. If we don't get to the fourth question more consistently, those students are going to be bored and will become disengaged. Let's really focus on more even allocation of our collaborative time next month."

In equity and excellence schools, leadership decisions about time extend to the classroom and individual students. The focus on student achievement is especially important in an environment where many students come to school with academic skills substantially below grade level. These schools typically display charts showing weekly improvements from the fall through the spring, giving the consistent message, *It's not how you start here that matters, but how you finish.* Improvements of more than one grade level in a single year are common, and teachers and administrators pay particular attention to students whose reading and writing deficiencies would have a profound impact on their success in other subjects. Some students spend as many as three hours per day in literacy interventions designed to get them to desired achievement levels. Leaders in equity and excellence schools know if a fifth-grade student is reading at a second-grade level, then there is no place for instructional strategies scattered among dozens of standards and curriculum strands. This student must learn to read, making up for years of reading deficiency, or the student will be headed for failure throughout his or her middle and high school years. Plus, the student will be almost certain to drop out as he or she fails to accumulate the required credits to graduate with peers.

Literacy is the top priority of equity and excellence schools, and leaders make it clear that the purpose of every lesson is to enhance student literacy skills. Teachers do not assign struggling readers to read a chapter and hope for the best. Rather, teachers have struggling students approach the text paragraph by paragraph, and then they stop the students and check for understanding, making marginal notes on paper or with the appropriate technology. Teachers prioritize comprehension over coverage. They also challenge the prevailing use of sustained silent reading because they know some students engage in little more than sustained silent *sitting* during this time. So, teachers frequently stop students as they read silently or aloud and check to ensure students have circled or highlighted unfamiliar vocabulary words, summarized every paragraph, and maximized every opportunity for improving literacy skills and personal confidence in reading. Teachers apply the same techniques in mathematics. Leaders and teachers understand that a significant problem in mathematics achievement concerns not merely number operations but also understanding the directions and stories in the mathematics test items.

Finally, a consistent finding in equity and excellence schools is that interventions occur during the school day. Although there are isolated examples of after-school and weekend programs having some effect, the consistent observation of equity and excellence teachers and leaders shows that students who most need intervention do not come to after-school and weekend sessions. Many students (and, indeed, teachers) have unbreakable obligations for sibling care, work, or other commitments outside school hours. If intervention is going to happen with any impact, equity and excellence schools conclude, it must happen *during* the school day.

Devoting Leadership Attention to Achievement

I have had the good fortune to shadow equity and excellence school leaders during their day. These leaders have no external similarities; they are young and old, less experienced and veterans, men and women, every color of skin, ebullient and reserved. But one thing they all have in common is they are frequently out of their offices and in the classrooms, hallways, and common areas of their schools. Even in the most heavily unionized environments, these leaders know they can walk into any class at any time, sit next to students, and learn about the reality of teaching and learning firsthand. It is equally important to note what these leaders are *not* doing. They are not answering email; in some cases, more than one hundred emails will accumulate when these leaders check their incoming mail. They are not answering their phone; rather, they have an assistant who respectfully but insistently explains to callers, "The principal has a commitment right now" to be with teachers and students. In what is perhaps the most telling decision of equity and excellence leaders, they do not attend many external meetings. At some risk to their relationships with central office department heads, equity and excellence principals decide that being fully present with students and faculty is more important than being visible in meetings. Every central office in every school system—even the very best ones I have observed—would benefit from an audit to critically evaluate the purposes and results of meetings. It is not unusual in some large systems for principals to be called out of the building two to three days each week, rendering their role as instructional leaders a frustrating impossibility. Unless the purpose of a meeting is deliberation and collaborative decision making, the goals of improved teaching and learning are far better served when the principal is in the school, not at meetings. This is particularly true when the purpose of the meetings is to deliver a message—a function that in the 21st century does not require in-person presentations.

Although every school needs an instructional leader, it is entirely possible the principal is not equipped to serve that purpose. If this is the case, then an assistant principal, dean, instructional coach, or other person can serve as the instructional leader and allow the principal to invest time in managing school operations and central office communication. But when the principal is the instructional leader, that function must take precedence over the vast majority of other claims on his or her time.

Building Strong Relationships

The evidence on the power of positive relationships among leaders and their colleagues is overwhelming (Ablon, 2018; Brown, 2018; Collins & Hansen, 2011). But while professional development conferences are full of elegies about the importance of relationships, equity and excellence leaders do more than echo the rhetoric of relationships. These leaders show their investment in relationships every day. They start with the faculty and staff, knowing their names, greeting them, and learning about their lives in and outside school. They know their students by name. Even in schools with eight hundred students or more, I am amazed at how principals greet students by name. They do this because they demand, even in the largest secondary schools where each teacher has upward of two hundred students, that every teacher do the same. They maintain portfolios showing not only the academic performance of each student but also something—at least one thing—about the life of the student outside school. Perhaps this tidbit of information is about a sport, personal interest, pet, sibling, or career goal. Relationships are not about hugs, although hugs are not necessarily a bad thing for some students who may never receive affirmation outside school. Rather, relationship building is about seeing the student or colleague as a person, not a statistic.

In several schools, I noticed the faculty labeled student data walls with the slogan, "Data Has a Face," and posted pictures of every student next to his or her row of data. These charts, with confidential data posted in the room where teachers meet to analyze data, reminded teachers and administrators that while they were focused on data and achievement, they must also consider the individual and emotional needs of every student. The pictures serve as a wonderful reminder that, although data analysis is a useful leadership tool, there are human beings behind the numbers, and leaders and teachers must never forget that.

Perhaps the most important part of building and maintaining relationships is the personal trust and credibility of the leader (Kouzes & Posner, 2011). Others may forgive leaders for errors in administration, data analyses, communication, and other flaws as long as those leaders maintain credibility with their colleagues. But if they lose credibility, their skills in analysis and communication are wasted. Some leaders believe because they are personally trustworthy and honest, they do not need to constantly tend to these essential elements of relationship building. That's a bad assumption. Because schools and educational systems are hierarchical institutions, and because people tend to distrust hierarchies and have perhaps had bad experiences with previous untrustworthy leaders, the building and maintenance of credibility requires leaders to put forth a continual effort. How do leaders build and maintain credibility? This requires a mantra of *promises made and promises kept*. At the beginning of every meeting, leaders should say, "At the last meeting, I promised I would _____, and I'm happy to tell you how I kept that promise." That should be a model for every collaborative team, department, cabinet, and, I would argue, board, and community meeting. When leaders set this example of credibility, they have a right to expect reciprocity. For example, "At our last meeting, we agreed everyone would bring a sample of proficient student work and a rubric to evaluate it. I'd like to do a quick reality check and celebrate that we are all keeping our promises."

When leaders lack a reserve of emotional and social capital, the descent into acrimony and cynicism can be quick and pervasive. But when leaders allocate their time and attention to what matters most (teaching and learning), build and maintain personal relationships with colleagues and students, and exhibit credibility at every turn, they build social capital they can draw on during the inevitable tough times. These leaders create an environment that, however challenging, is joyful, rewarding, and professionally satisfying for everyone who crosses the threshold of the schoolhouse door.

Summary

In this chapter, we considered the primary distinguishing characteristic of equity and excellence schools—a laser-like focus on student achievement. While nearly all schools claim to focus on student achievement, equity and excellence schools operationalize laser-like focus in very specific ways. It starts with visible indicators of student work on the walls and in trophy cases throughout the schools. These schools display not only data but also individual examples of terrific student essays, science projects, artwork, musical compositions, and personal goals. Leaders of equity and excellence schools also show calendar integrity; that is, how they invest time is a direct reflection of their values. They deliberately elevate time with students and teachers over the incessant demands of their role as administrators. They monitor collaborative team meetings and direct each team's focus on learning, assessment, intervention, and extension of learning for every student. Most important, equity and excellence leaders focus on relationships, knowing every student and staff member not merely as a pupil or employee but as a unique human being who deserves respect, attention, and an understanding that each has a life outside school.

In the next chapter, we consider how equity and excellence schools save time and improve student results through a rigorous process of collaborative scoring of student work and a collective commitment to student success.

CHAPTER 5

Conduct
Collaborative Scoring

Imagine your school's soccer team has a match at another school and, upon arriving, finds that the host team has changed the shape of the ball, the dimensions of the field, and the rules of the game. It's doubtful your students would (or should) participate because when the rules of the game are uncertain or change, it's impossible to have a fair game. Yet as crazy as that scenario may sound, it is precisely what happens in schools when students regularly have different standards of success, different criteria for evaluation, and different methods of grading every period of the day. Even within the same subject, different teachers can have significantly different evaluation policies, leaving students bewildered about what the expectations of their teachers really are.

It doesn't have to be that way. In experiments around the world—North and South America, Australia, Asia, Europe, and Africa, from 2005 through 2019—I have given teachers samples of anonymous work and asked them to evaluate the work with a scoring guide or rubric (see, for example, Reeves, 2016a). When teachers scored the rubrics alone, there was barely a 20 percent level of agreement. When they collaborated with colleagues, however, the level of agreement rose dramatically, to a consistency rate of more than 90 percent. Collaboration is not just about good feelings resulting from cooperation; it's about improving the quality and consistency of feedback to students. Researcher John Hattie (2012) provides compelling evidence from his synthesis of meta-analyses that feedback has an oversized impact on improving student achievement, but that impact is only as good as the quality of the feedback. If students find teacher scoring a mystery, they tend to ignore it, considering only the score and not paying much attention to how the teacher determined the score (Hattie, 2012). To encourage the highest levels of student achievement, teachers must lay the groundwork by providing students with both high-quality feedback and a fair scoring environment that allows them to reach their greatest potential.

This chapter presents a request for the same care in school that we expect on the playing field—fairness and consistency. In equity and excellence schools, this is a common expectation, and collaborative scoring is the norm. Sometimes scoring is formal, such as those from the original equity and excellence schools' scoring calibration conferences. I also noticed in equity and excellence schools that collaborative scoring sometimes occurs informally, with teachers simply asking a colleague over lunch or during a planning period, "Would you please take a look at this? I'd really appreciate another point of view on how I scored this student." Indeed, this idiosyncratic and informal communication among teachers is as important as the formal structures administrators sometimes attempt to impose. It is the *spirit* of collaboration, not merely the formal structure of collaboration, that matters.

This chapter will discuss several ways schools can incorporate collaborative scoring into their teaching practices. It will begin with an introduction to collaborative tasks and scoring guides before moving into a discussion of how collaborative scoring can improve quality and, critically, save teachers time in the long run. Next, we will delve into how educators can involve students in collaborative scoring through the use of a three-column rubric. Finally, we discuss the importance—and difficulty—of allowing oneself to be vulnerable in order to achieve the greatest benefits of collaborative scoring.

Beginning With Collaborative Tasks and Scoring Guides

In order to create effective assessments at any level—classroom, school, district, state, national, or provincial—we must begin with a clear set of learning expectations. Schools assess, for example, the ability of students to read and understand a paragraph, test a claim with evidence, plot lines on a graph, or draw inferences from scientific measurements. As a society, we have determined that such demonstrations of knowledge and skills are important for a successful citizenry. But the mere articulation of standards is insufficient. Developing effective assessments requires the translation of standards into performance tasks, and the translation of performance tasks into different levels of performance (Marzano, Norford, & Ruyle, 2019; Reeves, 2002b; Wiggins, 1998).

Once teachers establish performance tasks and a performance continuum, many are tempted to then administer these assessments to their students. By *performance continuum*, I mean explicit descriptions of student work that includes the following ranges of performance.

- **Not meeting standards:** That is, the student is not ready to approach the task. For example, if the lesson is on exponents, and the student does not understand multiplication, then the student is not ready to approach the exponent lesson without foundational support.

- **Progressing:** The student has a grasp of the task at hand but is not yet proficient. For example, if the proficiency standard is about supporting a claim with evidence, the "progressing" student has been able to express a claim and also some pieces of evidence but has not yet explicitly related how those pieces of evidence support or fail to support the claim.

- **Proficient:** This student performance meets all of the requirements for the standard. For example, if the standard required proficiency in scale, ratio, and the properties of regular and irregular polygons, the performance task might require the student to create an accurately labeled scale drawing of a school that contains rooms of different shapes.

- **Exemplary:** This represents work that is different in rigor and complexity. It is not merely "exceeding standards," as that label implies merely a quantitative distinction. Rather, the term "exemplary" implies a qualitative distinction in rigor and complexity. For example, building on the scale diagram used to demonstrate "proficient" performance in the previous paragraph, the "exemplary" student could create a three-dimensional model. That task is not merely "more" modeling at the two-dimensional level—a quantitative difference—but a different model that offers significantly greater cognitive challenges to the student. The student who was "proficient" in supporting a claim with evidence may show exemplary work by considering alternative evidence that supports and opposes the claim and then evaluating the credibility of each source.

However, the most important intermediary step is giving these tasks to a colleague and patiently waiting for him or her to struggle with directions that may seem perfectly appropriate for a fourth grader, but sometimes befuddle a colleague with a master's degree. One of the most insightful practices of equity and excellence schools is that colleagues are willing to ask their professional peers to complete a performance task. Only then can teachers confront the reality that directions, tasks, and rubrics, seemingly crystal clear in the eyes of the creator, are opaque or at least muddy when viewed through the eyes of a respected colleague. Students have no hope of engaging in a task if the expectations are unclear to their and other teachers. Thus, long before collaborative scoring takes place, collaborative development of tasks and scoring guides is essential. Teachers must first agree on what is expected and the levels of performance students might achieve on each task.

Improving Quality and Saving Time

Collaborative design of tasks and collaborative scoring of student work can strike teachers as time-consuming and frustrating chores, and so they are. But the evidence is clear—investing time in collaboration yields two key benefits: (1) improved quality of scoring and (2) saved time for teachers (Reeves, 2006). When I first provided samples of student work to teachers along with a scoring guide, they displayed almost no level of agreement, with one teacher claiming the student deserved a *4*—an exemplary rating—while a colleague insisted the same student work was "deplorable." As the author of what I believe were exquisitely designed scoring rubrics, I could have engaged in a full retreat, deciding my efforts were fruitless and that agreement was impossible. A more mature reaction, however, prevailed—I concluded these teachers were very capable and professional, and if they could not agree on what proficient student performance look like, then it was very unlikely that a nine-year-old would. Therefore, the reaction was not to have one colleague argue with another, as so often happens when scoring rubrics are accepted as "fixed," but rather to forge the essential conclusion that *the enemy is not each other; the enemy is ambiguity.* Thus, the teachers in my study collaborated to improve the clarity and specificity of the scoring guide, and then applied the revised product to a second set of student work samples (Reeves, 2006). The result was better, but still needed improvement. After four separate attempts to improve the quality of the scoring rubric, the level of agreement among the teachers rose to 92 percent—not perfect, but significantly better than their original efforts just a few hours before.

Collateral benefits of collaborative scoring are improved quality of scoring and student work, and also accelerated pace of scoring. As teachers score work collaboratively, the first work samples almost always yield disagreements. Perhaps the scoring guide had implicit exceptions clear to one teacher but not to another. Perhaps each teacher had expectations of the student work that were not part of the scoring guide but part of his or her general expectations for all student work. Working out these differences takes time, and early in the process it's easy for teachers to throw up their hands and say, "We'll never have time to score a complete classroom of work if we spent thirty minutes arguing over every piece of work!" That would be quite correct if collaborative efforts stop after one attempt. But every time I worked with groups of teachers to engage in three or four work samples consecutively, the frustrations of their first attempt gave way to their scoring becoming not only more consistent but also much, much faster.

As with any challenging professional task, collaborative scoring takes practice. Because teachers are used to being very good at their craft, the temptation is to give up when things do not come quickly and easily. But this is a task worth pursuing, as more practice yields higher-quality grading and better student work and saves teachers time.

Engaging Students in Collaborative Scoring With the Three-Column Rubric

Collaborative scoring is effective as a professional practice for teachers, but the benefits are compounded many times when students also become evaluators of their own and their peers' work. The best practice I have observed for engaging students in collaborative scoring is using the *three-column rubric* (see figure 5.1, page 50, for an example). The left-hand column identifies expectations for student performance in student-friendly language. The center column contains the student's self-assessment. The right-hand column includes the teacher's feedback regarding the student's self-assessment. This method ensures students understand the feedback and saves time for teachers who no longer need to write comments about student performance already obvious to the student. More important, it places the responsibility for reflection and assessment where it belongs—squarely on the shoulders of the learner. Teachers can use this rubric (see figure 5.1, page 50) for any grade level. Primary students might use simple *I can* statements, while secondary students use more elaborate multilevel rubrics. The key is that the language of the rubric must be accessible to students.

Most rubrics are designed for teachers and other evaluators to use. The student submits the work, the teacher grades it, and that's usually the end of the process. By contrast, in a three-column rubric, students take responsibility for assessing their own work, and teachers focus on those areas students are unclear about, whether proficient or not.

Using the three-column rubric engages students because they take on the powerful role of assessor. Teachers no longer have to write comments or provide rubric scores for every part of an assessment; they save time by focusing exclusively on student misunderstandings. When I have personally used this technique, the time required

My Work	Student Self-Assessment	Teacher Assessment
1. I accurately described the changes in each map, including new states and territories.	I made a three-column chart for 1800, 1830, and 1860, showing states and territories.	✓
2. I explained the reasons for changes in the maps.	I showed the laws that approved expansion.	Please expand your explanation to include wars, executive actions, and actions that were not authorized.
3. I explained at least two controversies about westward expansion.	I wrote a story about the Trail of Tears and summarized a debate on the Mexican-American War.	✓
4. I explained the impact of westward expansion on native nations.	I made a table showing the number of members of native nations who were killed and who died of disease.	Please expand your answer to include the loss of property and economic opportunity and the long-term consequences of displacement.

Figure 5.1: Sample three-column rubric.

to evaluate student work declined by more than 60 percent. I have heard similar anecdotal reports from teachers who have experimented with this idea. This not only saves teachers time but also gives students feedback much more quickly. Additionally, teacher feedback is not the final evaluation, but rather a method of improving student work in response to that feedback.

A variation on this theme is when students provide feedback to one another. Teachers in Cambridge, Massachusetts, and Dearborn, Michigan—respectively representing very high- and very low-socioeconomic status areas—engaged in the same practice as students by providing specific feedback to their colleagues using Google Docs (https://google.com/docs/about). Teachers evaluated students on the quality of their work *and* evaluated their colleagues on the quality, specificity, and helpfulness of the feedback they provided to their peers. This represents a quantum leap in the value of a group project. Instead of the typical situation in which students simply carve up the tasks to be done—hardly an example of collaboration—the individual and collective work required is significantly better than if they operated independently.

Showing Vulnerability

Among the many reasons people love teachers is that they are, other than immediate family members, our primary role models from a very early age. They are big, strong, kind, and wonderful. And they just know so much! Even as students progress from wide-eyed primary pupils to more skeptical adolescents, teachers remain important figures in the lives of every student. It is, therefore, not easy for an educated professional that students revere and colleagues admire to admit struggling to decode the directions or scoring guides for a fourth-grade mathematics assessment. It's not easy for people with advanced English degrees to consider that a colleague might have a better way to score an essay. Our expertise is part of who we are as professionals and people, and nobody likes their professional and personal identity challenged. Yet, this vulnerability is essential if collaborative scoring is to reach its potential. Teachers must admit when directions they believe are clear may not be as clear as they thought. They need to acknowledge when the guidelines for scoring an assignment a student teacher accepted without a whisper of challenge may not be so clear to a friend and colleague with decades of experience in the classroom. It would be naïve not to accept that when the very heart of our authority as teachers—how we evaluate student work—is challenged, it might hurt a bit. Rather than pretend vulnerability is just part of the job and that we need to get over it, we need to accept this element of collaborative scoring is worthy of discussion.

Schools can take certain steps to reduce the unwanted side effects of vulnerability. For example, collaborative teams can begin by using anonymous student work, with no clue about the identity of the student or teacher. The only things that matter are the work itself and the scoring guide. In addition, teams can begin this process with rubrics from third-party sources, such as state or provincial department of education websites or, where applicable, Advanced Placement (AP) or International Baccalaureate (IB) websites. Because the identities of the student and teacher are unknown and the rubric author is no one in the school, it is possible to ask penetrating questions about how to improve the directions and scoring guide. The final key to the effective use of vulnerability is to ask students to apply the rubrics themselves. The fatal flaw with many commercially produced rubrics, as well as those from state or provincial websites and those of testing companies, is one assessment expert writes them for another assessment expert—not for students who must understand them. The test of any rubric is for teachers to understand and apply it consistently *and* for students to use it. That means teachers—the authority figures in the school—must be willing to take action when a student says, "I have no idea what you expect me to do," even after teachers have written what they think is a magnificently clear rubric. Only after the student has clarity surrounding the task and scoring process can teachers expect to see achievement increase.

Summary

In this chapter we explored a key professional practice of equity and excellence schools—collaborative scoring of student work. We began by considering the rationale for collaborative scoring. In order for students to actively engage in their education, they must believe the feedback they receive is fair. Fairness is a function of *consistency*—the same performance yields the same or very similar feedback from teachers. When teachers agree to look at the same piece of student work, apply the same scoring guide alone, and then together, to assess that work, they can identify inconsistencies in scoring that can potentially rob students of effective feedback. When different teachers have different success criteria, or when they apply the same criteria in different ways, students are left wondering how to improve. Students may make excuses for why they received a low mark on an assignment ("The teacher doesn't like me"), rather than saying with clarity, "I didn't have enough supporting details in my second paragraph, and I had a weak conclusion, but now I know how to make it better next time." When teachers score collaboratively, variation is greatly reduced and communication with students is vastly improved.

Collaborative scoring not only improves the quality of feedback from teachers to students but also saves teachers time. In studies of teachers scoring student work, I find the more frequently collaborative scoring conferences take place, the faster teachers are able to grade the same assignment, reducing the time required to grade an assignment by more than 70 percent (Reeves, 2006). This chapter continued with an invitation for students to participate with teachers as assessors of their own work and the work of their peers.

Finally, the chapter concluded with the observation that collaboration requires *vulnerability*; that is, the willingness to share what has traditionally been private and personal work—evaluating students—with colleagues who may have different opinions. As educators, we are accustomed to being right, being the expert in the room, and having everyone accept and respect our professional judgments. When a colleague expresses a different point of view, it can feel not only like a professional disagreement but also like a personal attack on our identity as experts. This is why it is absolutely vital for leaders to create an emotionally safe environment that allows collaborative teams to work together, disagree, find common ground, and move on with goodwill. The next chapter particularly addresses this presumption of goodwill and respect for professional expertise and discusses a commitment by all teachers to nonfiction writing.

CHAPTER 6

Emphasize Nonfiction Writing

When observing the writing portfolios in schools with high poverty and low achievement, I noticed something important. While the teachers were asking students to write, most of that writing was fiction, fantasy, personal narratives, and poetry. A good deal of it was very low rigor, such as acrostics in which a Valentine's Day poem would consist of nothing more than thinking of words that begin with *V-A-L-E-N-T-I-N-E*. Although students might have the ability to engage in some poetic expression, alliteration, rhyming, vivid imagination, and onomatopoeia, we never know because the teacher never asks. When I counted the types of student writing, the ratio of fiction, fantasy, and personal narrative to nonfiction was more than ninety to one. By contrast, in schools with similar demographics and high performance, I find a balance between fiction and nonfiction. There is room for poetry, fantasy, and narrative, of course, but these teachers also include writing to describe, compare, and evaluate. The scarcity of nonfiction writing is pervasive, especially in secondary schools, where classes outside of English language arts often provide assessments that focus exclusively on multiple choice or short-answer items. The exceptions are classes designed for the highest-performing students, such as those taking classes in the International Baccalaureate and Advanced Placement curricula. There, one finds writing in history, economics, psychology, science, and mathematics. However, Graham (2019) makes the powerful point that nonfiction writing is strongly associated with student success in these disciplines, a finding that is strikingly similar to my own findings (Reeves, 2002a).

This chapter discusses the critical importance of encouraging students to write nonfiction text across all disciplines. First, we explore some of the main objections educators may face when encouraging nonfiction writing before concluding with a solution to one of these objections—a method for simplifying scoring rubrics for cross-disciplinary use.

Dealing With Objections to Nonfiction Writing

The most common objection to requesting students engage in more nonfiction writing is the same objection raised to any change in professional practices in education: "We don't have the time." Although this objection is common, it doesn't make much sense because, after all, all teachers have the same number of hours in the day and roughly the same number of hours in the school day. The question is not one of available time, but rather how to allocate time. As the previous chapter on collaboration suggested, time allocated to collaborative scoring of writing assignments not only improves the accuracy and consistency of scoring but also improves the speed with which teachers engage in this complex task. These improvements require practice, and practice requires time—time provided by administrators who give time for collaborative assessment during their staff meetings and department meetings. Teachers are overburdened with curriculum and other demands on their day. State and provincial standards are notoriously voluminous. Even the Common Core State Standards, which promised to be more focused than their predecessors, create the fatal assumption that every student needs to gain only one year of learning; in reality, many students need two or more years of learning to catch up to their present grade level. The only alternatives facing teachers are to either devote more hours of the day to academic instruction or cover fewer standards. Thus, the expectation that students gain proficiency in nonfiction writing seems to be just one more diversion from the need to cover the standards students will be tested on.

Essentially, this objection is not a lack of time, but rather, "If I devote time to nonfiction writing, then I will not have time to cover the necessary curriculum in mathematics, science, and social studies, and my students' scores in those subjects will decline." This hypothesis (that more time devoted to nonfiction writing will lead to lower test scores in academic subject areas) can be expressed in a graph (see figure 6.1) in which the horizontal axis is the frequency of nonfiction writing and the vertical axis is academic proficiency in mathematics, science, reading, and social studies. If the hypothesis is correct, we would expect to see a line that goes from the upper left to the lower right, suggesting that with each increase in the frequency of nonfiction writing, scores in other subjects decline.

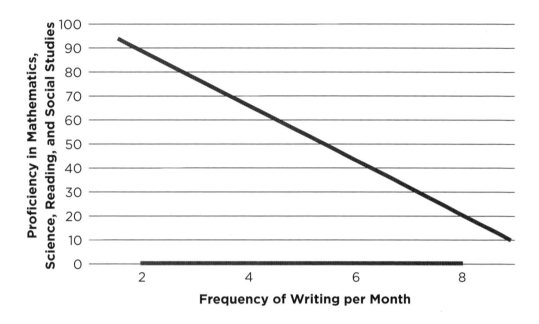

Source: Adapted from Reeves, 2002a.

Figure 6.1: The hypothesis—more time on writing means lower scores in academic subjects.

However, the actual student performance data I accumulated from elementary, middle, and high school students from four different states at the school, district, and state or province level shows student achievement (represented by the line on the graph) is precisely the opposite of the hypothesis (see figure 6.2, page 58). So, as the frequency of nonfiction writing increases, student performance in other subjects increases (Reeves, 2002a).

To be sure, the relationship is imperfect. In statistical terms, it hovers between 0.7 and 0.8, meaning in some cases there are high-achieving students who do not engage in much nonfiction writing, and there are low-achieving students who do lots of nonfiction writing. But overall, the relationship is compelling: more nonfiction writing is associated with strong student performance in every other academic area. It is also important to acknowledge that *correlation* is not *causation*. These graphs do not demonstrate nonfiction writing caused improved student achievement.

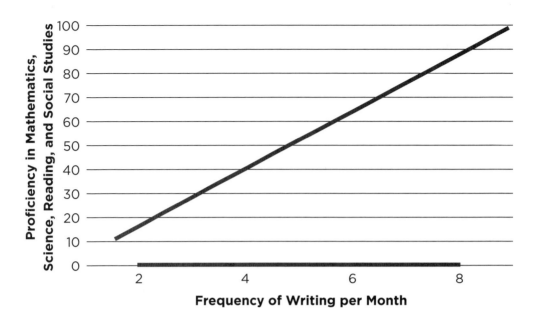

Source: Adapted from Reeves, 2002a.

Figure 6.2: The reality—more time on writing is associated with higher scores in academic subjects.

However, what correlations can do is to disprove the hypothesis in figure 6.1 (page 57), conclusively undermining the contention that more nonfiction writing hurts academic performance in other areas.

Finally, there is a frequent objection about the writing sequence in students' literacy development. Traditionally, language development is linear—first students learn to speak, then to read, and then to write. If they are having difficulty speaking or reading, then teachers should delay writing instruction, especially for students whose primary language is not English. However, the opposite may be true. Writing provides students time to think, reflect, and express themselves at their own pace in a way that asking questions directly or forcing students to read aloud cannot. Let them write! Let them express themselves at their own pace, in their own way, and with the quiet confidence that comes from having the luxury of time to formulate an answer rather than feeling impatient glares thrown at them. Language development is holistic, not linear, and giving students the opportunity to write—even at very young ages—allows them to describe their ideas and images in meaningful ways and that, most important, builds their confidence as writers, readers, and speakers (Calkins, 1994, 2019).

Simplifying Scoring Rubrics for Cross-Disciplinary Writing

The evolution of scoring guides, or rubrics, for writing was a backlash against the ambiguity prevailing when teachers award a grade such as B+ or 87 on a piece of student work. The student is left without a clue as to how the teacher reached this judgment. Before the common use of scoring guides, it was not unusual for a teacher to simply say, "I know good writing when I see it," and assume (like factory workers in the 20th century) it was the students' job to submit the work and (like foremen in those factories) it was the teacher's job to evaluate the work. Scoring rubrics, however elegant and sophisticated they may be, only teachers (and not students) use are little better than the factory model because the evaluation of student work remains a mystery. The gold standard in rubric design is whether students can use the rubric to evaluate their own work and, as a result of this self-evaluation, reflect on and improve the quality of their work without waiting for the teacher's judgment.

Some of the greatest gains in overall student achievement have taken place in schools that commit to nonfiction writing in every subject, every grade, every month (Graham, 2019; Reeves, 2002a). To make this commitment accessible to teachers whose expertise is not English language arts, it is helpful for the faculty to agree on the use of a single scoring rubric for every teacher within a grade level or span of grade levels and irrespective of the subject. This rubric is necessarily less complex and lengthy than typical rubrics, such as the commonly used six-trait rubric for writing. Teachers could use a truncated scoring guide such as the following in a middle school (grades 6–8) in every subject.

1. **Not meeting standards:** The reader is unable to make sense of the writing because it is illegible or the words don't make sense. The writing does not respond to the teacher's prompt.

2. **Progressing:** The writing is legible and sentences are complete, start with a capital letter, and end with appropriate punctuation. The grammar is mostly correct, and the writing progresses clearly with a beginning, middle, and end. The writing responds to the teacher's prompt.

3. **Proficient:** All criteria for progressing are met, plus the sentences include key supporting details. Each paragraph has a topic sentence and clear conclusion. If there are multiple paragraphs, there are clear transitions from one paragraph to the next. If the writer is using external evidence or quotations, he or she includes the name, date, and source of the quotation.

4. **Exemplary:** All criteria for proficient are met, plus the writing includes rich and powerful vocabulary. The writer not only responds to the teacher's prompt but also offers additional explanations, details, evidence, and arguments that help the reader understand the author's work.

Elementary school teachers will probably want to use different student-accessible language and may wish to use *I can* statements, particularly for primary grades, such as, "I can start every sentence with a capital letter." High school teachers may wish to make the rubric somewhat more complex, though I caution against too much complexity. The critical test for any writing rubric is the degree students can, without the aid of the teacher, apply the rubric to their own writing and make revisions that strengthen the writing without teacher supervision and intervention.

When I say schools with high achievement commit to nonfiction writing in *every subject, every grade*, that is precisely what I mean. The point is not to divert time and attention from subjects other than English language arts, but to deepen students' understanding through the deep thinking writing requires. Examples include the following.

- **Mathematics:** Review the *x-y* graph you created from the chart. Make a prediction about what would happen to the values on the *y*-axis if you extend the *x*-axis to the right. Explain your answer.

- **Social studies:** Consider the two maps of the United States—one from 1800 and the second from 1859. Describe the differences in the two maps, and explain the events that led to those differences.

- **Music:** Reflect on this week's rehearsals. How did your singing (or playing) change during the week? How did singing (or playing) of the others in your ensemble change? Please explain how these changes helped or hindered your musical performance.

- **Science:** This week we studied refraction of light. Where else do you notice refraction taking place? Please describe the setting, and speculate about the causes for the refractions you see. What colors do you see? What colors in the spectrum do you not see?

- **Art:** Select any work of Pablo Picasso that especially moves you and explain why. Speculate about what Picasso is attempting to express in this piece of art.

- **Technology:** Explain how a single error in one line of coding might make a significant difference in the functioning of a program. Please illustrate with an example.

- **Business:** We have learned about the fundamental parts of a balance sheet—assets, liabilities, and equity. Are there important parts of a business not reflected in the balance sheet? If so, please explain what is missing. If not, explain why the balance sheet represents a complete description of the business.

We should think of writing as *thinking through the end of a pen*. While there may be arguments about the value of writing, I doubt anyone would challenge the value of thinking about math, science, social studies, and, for that matter, art, music, and sports. All of these vital disciplines are worth thinking about, and therefore, I would argue, worth writing about.

Summary

Students who write are students who think—making arguments, describing the beautiful and the terrible, comparing truth to assertion, and expressing their understanding of the world around them. Their world can be the flower or toad grasping the attention of a kindergartener or the application of a trimetric function in high school. High-performing, high-poverty schools regularly expect students to write to describe, persuade, compare, and evaluate. There is room for fantasy, fiction, and poetry, but a distinguishing characteristic of these schools is that nonfiction writing as a tool for thinking is not optional.

When this technique is applied to maximum effect, every subject in every grade requires writing. The suggestions for writing prompts in this chapter are just a beginning, and the creativity of teachers and students will vastly expand the repertoire of writing prompts teachers can use in engaging and exciting ways in their classrooms. Writing, as with any subject, is insufficient if it is merely mentioned in the curriculum but never transferred to classroom practice. In order for a curriculum to come alive, students and teachers must have a regular system of formative assessment that allows students to understand, with careful coaching and support, how to improve. That is the subject of the next chapter.

CHAPTER 7

Utilize Frequent Formative Assessment With Multiple Opportunities for Success

Formative assessment is, at its core, a type of feedback teachers must consider in context. Although feedback can be an exceptionally powerful strategy for helping students understand the difference between their current performance and the desired performance, there is a wide spectrum of quality when it comes to feedback. Moreover, in education, the term *formative* is widely misused, with test vendors labeling any test that does not happen at the end of the year *formative*, in contrast to the *summative* end-of-year assessments.

In this chapter, we will consider the critical distinction between tests that are mere exercises in compliance and those that are genuinely formative because, as the name suggests, they inform teaching and learning. We discuss the assertion that if we really use formative assessments to help students improve, it follows logically that students should be able to demonstrate their improvement by taking the assessments again. We address the oft-asked question from frustrated teachers—How many retakes are enough?—and then consider how to strike the balance between allowing students the opportunities they need to display success and ensuring they don't simply avoid trying at the first assessment opportunity by proposing the menu solution.

Harnessing Feedback as the Most Powerful Tool for Improved Performance

All of us receive feedback throughout our lives. Some of the feedback is abrupt, such as the many physical falls to the ground we endured after attempting our first steps. Some of the feedback is harsh, such as the disapproving glares and words from parents and other authority figures when disapproving our actions. Some of the feedback is bewildering and frightening, such as the screeches from parents on the sidelines of children's athletic contests. But sometimes, if we're lucky, we experience feedback so effective that, within minutes, we can apply that feedback and watch our performance improve.

Perhaps a parent, older sibling, or teacher, as we struggled to read our first words, helped us sound out *cat* letter by letter. *C* is "cuh," *a* is "ah," and *t* is "tuh"—"Now you do it: *cuh, ah, tuh . . . cat!*" This process was repeated endlessly, patiently, interspersed with praise and joyful surprise each time we successfully completed a word, then a phrase, and then a sentence. Columbia University professor Lucy M. Calkins (1983) expresses this joy of learning and teaching in a tender moment described in *Lessons From a Child*, when observers note how a particular child must possess some exceptional gift for literacy. Calkins (1983) assures the observer the student is indeed gifted, as are all the students in the class because they have found the inestimable joy of reading and writing.

Although all these events constitute feedback, there are specific criteria for high-quality feedback strongly associated with gains in learning. Hattie (2012) infers from his synthesis of meta-analyses that feedback is one of the most powerful techniques teachers have when it comes to improving student results. To put the power of feedback in context, Hattie (2012) uses the measurement of effect size. The term *effect size*, usually represented with the lowercase *d*, offers readers a way of synthesizing many different studies into a single expression of impact. For example, an effect size of .4 equates to about a year of learning, and therefore educational interventions with an effect size of 1.2 have a very strong impact, while those with an effect size of .1 or .2 may have the property of statistical significance, but pale in comparison of their impact to other impacts that have much higher effect sizes. For example, socioeconomic status, a variable most people regard as particularly influential in student learning, has an effect size of 0.59. Effective feedback, by contrast, has an effect size more than three times greater than socioeconomic status. This does not mean poverty is irrelevant; indeed, by Hattie's (2012) calculations, their respective wealth or poverty effects students by a gain or loss of about a year of learning. The inference from Hattie's (2012) analysis is not that poverty is unimportant, for it is an extremely important variable related to student learning. Rather, the inference is that what teachers do—particularly when it comes to providing effective feedback—is also important, and perhaps even more important than the socioeconomic status of students.

Although feedback is a powerful influence on student learning, there is a wide variation in feedback quality and effectiveness. Consider feedback on a continuum, from the gentle, immediate, and specific feedback of the person who taught us to read at one end, to the indecipherable screams of parents who exhort their six-year-olds to "Play defense!" at the other. Then, consider four criteria for feedback most likely to improve student learning. An easy way to place feedback along this continuum is the acronym *FAST*, which stands for *fair, accurate, specific,* and *timely* (Reeves, 2016b).

The essence of *fairness* is consistency. Perhaps you have witnessed Olympic ice skating or gymnastics competitions where judges, all looking at the same performance, mark the athletes quite differently. Imagine if, closer to home, students playing soccer, football, rugby, or baseball—any sport with boundaries—wandered close to the boundary line, and one official signaled the player was in bounds, another contended the player was out of bounds, and a third official kept the spectators waiting as he scratched his head in bewilderment. Whatever the ultimate judgment, spectators on both sides would shout, "That's not fair!" because they expect adults in charge of the game to come to a consistent conclusion about the boundaries of the field and the positions of the athletes on it. Although certainly officials do disagree from time to time, the general expectation is that they apply the rules of the game consistently. Players and spectators can accept it when a call goes against their team. What they cannot abide is inconsistency and their consequent inability to understand the officials' judgment.

Fairness for student feedback poses similar expectations. When a piece of work from one student earns a smiley face with the annotation, "Good job!" from one teacher, and the same piece of work is returned full of corrections from another teacher, the student is understandably confused. As students progress to more advanced subjects at higher grade levels (and the syllabi and accompanying policies become more voluminous), the inconsistencies and consequent lack of fairness remains the same. High school students can have seven different classes with seven radically different feedback policies and procedures in a single day. It is as if they are attending a soccer tournament where each game has a different ball, field dimensions, and rules. Eventually, the students stop playing the game. But in equity and excellence schools, a solid commitment to fairness keeps students engaged. The feedback can be negative or positive, but students know it is fair, and thus they are willing to invest the energy to apply that feedback to improve their performance.

The most effective way to ensure that feedback is fair—that is, consistent—is the collaborative scoring process that we considered in a previous chapter (chapter 5, page 45). I do not underestimate that collaboration can be challenging, as all of us can be very proprietary about our own grading and feedback mechanisms. One effective and respectful way to address these concerns is to proactively offer feedback not with the work of our own students but with anonymous student work. In schools and systems with several classes of the same grade, teachers can exchange a set of twenty papers, with the names of students, teachers, and schools removed. Therefore, in this collaborative process, the only comparison is of the student work to the common expectations of the teachers. There is no possibility of a reference to "my students" for "my class" because the identities of the students and teachers are unknown. In very small schools where there are singleton teachers—that is, only one teacher for a particular grade or subject—the website AllThingsPLC.info offers contact information for teachers in similar circumstances with whom singleton teachers can communicate.

The second criterion for effective feedback is it must be *accurate*. However obvious this criterion may seem, an astonishing amount of feedback in schools is inaccurate. Teachers know this well, having been on the receiving end of feedback from evaluators who do not understand the classroom context. For example, an observer may note a teacher "lacks classroom management skills" based simply on an observation that a student left class without permission, when in reality the student may be suffering from a medical condition and might have prearranged permission from the teacher to leave class when necessary. Such a situation is somewhat familiar. However, teachers not only receive inaccurate feedback but also deliver it, sometimes concluding a student lacks skills in mathematics when, for example, the student's primary challenge is reading unfamiliar English-language instructions on a mathematics test. The essence of accuracy in providing feedback is a clear link between what we observe, the feedback we provide, and the reality of the performance we are assessing. An example of the practical application of the principle of accuracy is the use of two-column mathematics assessments. When I was teaching middle school mathematics, two-thirds of my students did not speak English at home. I therefore needed to understand which student errors were based upon misconceptions in mathematics and which errors were related to their lack of familiarity with the English language. In a ten-item assessment, five items would have only numbers, letters, and symbols. Another five items would have the same mathematical challenges embedded into story problems. Any difference in the performance of these different types of items would allow me to accurately assess the degree to which I needed to focus on improving mathematics skills or improving English literacy skills. This technique, I should add, is valuable not only in the context of students who are not speaking English at home but for many students for whom the terminology of mathematics story problems may be unfamiliar.

The third criterion for effective feedback is that it must be *specific*. This is the opposite of the bewildered child parents tell to "Play defense!" when there might be dozens of specific actions effective defensive play might entail. Similarly, when the teacher tells a student to "Be more careful!" or "Show your work!" that student may have no idea what specific elements of his or her performance the teacher expects to change. My maternal grandmother was a concert pianist in her youth and could doubtless provide a thousand pieces of advice as I attempted a Chopin étude or Bach prelude. But she would invariably focus on a single note or phrase, just as a great athletic coach might focus solely on a foot, hand, or head position, rather than all the things an athlete might improve all at once. Rather than saying, "Write neatly!" a teacher might better suggest students form just three similar letters—*b*, *p*, and *d*—more neatly. After students have practiced those letters to perfection, the teacher might progress to others. Rather than express our frustration with the exasperated command to "Show your work!" we might be better advised to ask, "What is the question this problem is asking?" and only when that question has been answered, ask, "What is the first piece of information we need to know?" I heard a student of famed violinist Itzhak Perlman explain that he might spend an entire lesson on a single phrase. While a concerto might consist of thousands of phrases, the maestro's aim was to provide feedback so specific that, ultimately, the student would be able to analyze a misstep, break it down into its smallest parts, and then correct his or her performance, note by note, phrase by phrase. Authors and educational consultants Robert Eaker and Janel Keating (2015) advocate this technique when they advise teachers to avoid the generic pursuit of proficiency on a standard in favor of incremental progress on each skill. Effective feedback, in sum, requires specificity.

The fourth criterion for effective feedback is *timely*. When toddlers are learning to walk, they do not receive a lecture at the end of the day explaining the mechanics of human locomotion. Bumps, stumbles, and falls occur every few seconds. Effective teachers of writing do not pour a sea of red ink onto a student's paper at the end of the semester, but rather help students to construct, deconstruct, and reconstruct just the right words, phrases, sentences, and paragraphs in real time. Consider the chorus teacher who, within seconds or minutes, identifies the wrong notes, dynamics, and phrasing, and then skillfully guides students to fix every deficiency immediately. An observer can hear improvements in student performance within a ten-minute span. Mathematics, science, social studies, and literacy teachers should aspire to provide feedback as timely as their colleagues in the music department and get results they can see and hear within a single class period. Some of the best models for timely feedback occur during athletic practices, where coaches routinely provide feedback that is immediate and precise. They would never wait until the next day, nor would they encourage students to just "work harder," but rather they provide feedback that is timely, as well as consistent, accurate, and specific. Similarly, students need not struggle at home with a page full of problems that are bewildering. Instead, they can receive timely feedback with effective practice sessions that happen in the middle of class. Whether teachers use electronic response systems or whiteboards on which students write their answers with erasable markers, students can receive timely feedback within minutes of attempting each problem.

Ensuring Formative Assessment Is Formative

One of the most popular education trends is the use of formative assessment. Unfortunately, much of this assessment is decidedly uninformative. The reason is not because school leaders and teachers lack good intentions, but a failure to provide the time, leadership, training, and collaboration essential to ensure the formative assessment is successful. As a result, two schools can use identical assessments but have dramatically different results. In the first school, the assessment yields information that guides improved teaching and leadership decisions. In the second, the assessment yields the same information, but constraints on time and attention force teachers and leaders to ignore the information and, thankful that the assessment intrusion has passed, continue current practices.

The late educator Grant Wiggins (1998) propelled formative assessment into the consciousness of educators in the 1990s. He distinguished between assessment *of* learning (summative assessment), assessment *for* learning (formative assessment), and assessment *as* learning (daily classroom practice). DuFour et al. (2016) popularized the term *common formative assessment* in the context of PLCs by focusing on the four critical questions.

1. What do we want students to learn?

2. How will we know if they have learned it?

3. What will we do if they have not learned it?

4. What will we do if they have already learned it?

Collaborative teams of teachers in a PLC cannot satisfactorily address the second of these questions without using common formative assessments. Author and presenter Larry Ainsworth (2004) integrates standards, curriculum, and assessment into a coherent system. Hattie's (2009, 2012) groundbreaking research analyzing more than 250 million students confirms that formative assessment has a profoundly positive impact on student achievement. Still, education leaders and policymakers face a central challenge: assessment is *formative* because of how teachers and school leaders choose to use it. Schools are making huge investments in assessments, but the return depends not merely on the quality of the test or dazzling technology but also on the teaching and leadership decisions that accompany it. Maximizing the value of formative assessment requires leaders to shift from observation to insight, from effects to causes, and from impressions to impact.

To implement effective formative assessments in every classroom, teachers and leaders must have time to analyze data. This is a straightforward process in which teachers understand the concepts that the students understand and those concepts that must be retaught. They also use this analysis to understand which specific students need intervention and support and which students require learning extensions. Technology makes it easy to observe student performance, but insight into the link between teaching and learning is much more difficult. Insight is not merely "looking at data," as so many schools claim to do. Insight requires evidence from collaborative teams of professionals linking specific student results data to specific teaching and leadership practices. When someone says, "Mathematics scores are low," he or she is merely looking at data. Insightful teachers and leaders use data to *inform* instruction: "Our students are doing well in arithmetic but not so well in story problems. This suggests that we need to be more deliberate about understanding the questions. So, next week I'm going to insert a check for understanding in every story problem and ask students to rephrase the question and also draw a picture to illustrate the problem. Before they start trying to solve the mathematics problem, I'll know if they have correctly understood the question." These differences are not esoteric or philosophical but matters of specific practice—practices in high-performing schools that other schools can replicate. High-performing schools' success is not about the programs they buy, but the practices they pursue.

It's tempting to assess leadership and teaching performance based on impressions. People have admired inspirational rhetoric since the time of Demosthenes, the master Greek orator who, according to legend, practiced speeches with rocks in his mouth. But history teaches us there is a profound difference between those who speak well and those who inspire action. When Demosthenes finished an oration, the people said, "How well he spoke." But when the fearless, if less eloquent, Roman senator Cicero spoke, the people said, "Let us march." We should be skeptical of leaders and teachers whose oratorical skills mask their impact (or lack of impact) on students.

I have delivered Demosthenic lessons. My students were amused and impressed, but a later objective analysis of their learning revealed I failed in my teaching. Analysis of formative assessment data forced me to confront the differences between what I aspired to achieve with students and what they actually learned. The best leaders will likewise use formative assessment not as a hammer to embarrass teachers but as a lever to prod even the best and most experienced to improve their practices. Harvard University physics professor Eric Mazur (1997) was an award-winning lecturer but decided to dramatically change his approach to teaching by having students respond to problems in class (rather than in their dorm rooms) and thus receive immediate feedback from their peers and the teacher. He sacrificed his award-winning eloquence in the service of student learning.

Formative assessment can be exceptionally powerful. When resources and time are constrained, board members and educational leaders should allocate scarce resources to strategies with the greatest potential to impact student achievement. For formative assessment to be successful, leaders must insist that administrators and teachers move beyond observation to insight, from understanding of effects to analysis of causes, and from impressions to impact.

Avoiding Over-Testing and Under-Assessing

The suggestion for frequent formative assessment is often met with the objection, "But our students are over-tested already! How can you justify spending more time on assessments when I need time to teach?" This challenge must be taken seriously, as teachers' time is a precious resource we must respect. This concern deserves some scrutiny. In U.S. states with even the most demanding end-of-year assessments, there are about four instructional days devoted to testing. With a 180-day school year, this testing is only 2.2 percent of the school year. With many annual school budgets exceeding $100 million, it is reasonable to spend four days evaluating whether or not schools invested those dollars wisely. The concerns I hear from teachers, however, are about the cumulative effect of tests throughout the year; it's not just the four days of state tests but also the district-mandated formative assessments every six to eight weeks, some of which require two class periods or more. That's another eight days on top of the state-required four days. Some schools also require additional tests, as often as weekly. In these situations, the complaints from teachers about over-testing seem justified.

We must, therefore, distinguish between *testing*—the educational equivalent of the autopsy—and *assessment*—the educational equivalent of the physical examination. Autopsies can be revealing, but they never do the patient, who lies lifeless on the examining table, much good. Physical exams, by contrast, can be immensely valuable, allowing patients to adjust lifestyle, medications, and treatments to prolong their lives and improve the quality of their years. Formative assessment, used wisely, provides similar information for students and teachers. Formative assessment data let educators know if they need to change the schedule to allow essential interventions to support vital skills, or conduct further testing to qualify students for support for special education or English language learning. For the vast majority of students, these assessments provide deep insight about how they can close the gap between their present levels of performance and their goal of meeting or exceeding grade-level performance. When formative assessment is truly *formative*—it informs teaching and learning—each assessment is part of the learning cycle that includes performance, feedback, assessment, and more feedback and reassessment. For most students, this virtuous cycle leads to improved motivation and learning. But it would be naïve not to acknowledge that reassessment may demotivate some students. Teachers in an environment where reassessment is the norm can become frustrated, asking, "How many retakes are enough?"

Considering How Many Retakes Are Enough

When I first published the results of the equity and excellence schools, I was careful to explain that multiple opportunities for learning did not mean infinite opportunities for learning (Reeves, 2004). Some students will find the cycle of performance, assessment, and feedback useful for improved achievement, and this is what we see in great musical, athletic, and artistic performances. Fifty rough drafts of a painting, a dozen rough drafts of a story, or scores of repetitions for the athlete seem normal, provided each increment of performance yields an equal increment of improvement. However, improved performance is not a sufficient motivator for some students. These students incessantly ask, "Does it count?" and, if the answer is *no,* they decide, "The juice isn't worth the squeeze," so to speak. Why work hard now, they reason, if we can delay the pain of exertion for another day? It is difficult to imagine a marathon runner saying, "The race isn't for three months. Why run today if no one is watching?" A violinist is unlikely to wait until the night before the performance to practice, reasoning, "No one applauds for a rehearsal, so why work hard now?" However, unlike in athletics or musical performance, the practical reality of the classroom is that this sort of motivational calculus happens all the time.

Although some schools subscribe to the model of infinite retakes of assessments, projects, and papers, I would suggest an alternative that preserves the essence of the principles of formative assessment while respecting the legitimate concerns of teachers who face barrels full of papers, projects, and tests the last week of the semester. The *one-retake rule* respects the role of the teacher in providing feedback and the students who, for many reasons, may not have given their best on the first try. Home lives can be chaotic. Students have jobs. Family demands, including sibling care and, more commonly, care for adults, preclude the home environment from being conducive to study and homework. More critically, teacher feedback is valuable but almost always ignored in a no-retake environment. The one-retake rule allows for the challenges of life to occur while giving students the chance to maximize feedback. My system was to award, on a one-hundred-point assignment, fifty points for the first draft and fifty points for the second. The operating presumption is that the first test, paper, or project would be flawed and that student performance would benefit from my feedback. Thus, a second effort was not only allowed but also required. In the unlikely event that a student demonstrated mastery on the first draft, which was eligible for only fifty points of credit, I could mark it, "One hundred points—no rewrite required." Word spread like wildfire that the way to succeed in my class was to do it right the first time. For the most part, the cycle of working hard, submitting the work, getting specific feedback, and then resubmitting the work seemed to be effective. But that was it—one retake, not endless retakes. What if students fail to demonstrate proficiency on the second retake? The answer, I have found, is the menu solution.

Implementing the Menu Solution

Some students claim to just be bad test-takers. Although I doubt this is true—test-taking is a skill, like walking, playing video games, or listening before speaking—I acknowledge that some students consider it their role to test adult authority by insisting they just can't get the job done, even after two opportunities to do so. The answer that has worked for me and for many teachers is the *menu solution* (Reeves, 2016a). The challenge—to demonstrate proficiency on a set of academic standards—does not change, but there are more ways to demonstrate proficiency than performance on a test. For example, in a social studies class, students could demonstrate their knowledge on a traditional test and, failing that, get feedback, study more, and retake the exam. But after that, students could then choose from a menu. If the unit considered student understanding of simile and metaphor, students could simply take a unit test. But, failing that and the retake, they could find examples of simile and metaphor in an appropriate fictional text or newspaper article. They could write their own short story, employing at least five examples of simile and metaphor. They could consider the proposition that "metaphor is a more powerful way to describe a character than simile" and use contrasting examples to support or oppose the proposition. All options from the menu have two things in common. First, they require students to exhibit a deep understanding of the concepts in question and thus demonstrate proficiency in the assessed standards. Second, they are significantly more rigorous and difficult than simply performing well on the test. The menu solution, in sum, is not the easy way out, but a challenging alternative.

Summary

Formative assessment is only truly *formative* if it informs teaching and learning. Administrators and teachers must, therefore, be wary of labels, knowing that *formative* means nothing if teachers and leaders do not have the time to immediately apply the insights from these assessments to modify and improve both teaching and learning. School leaders who advocate formative assessments must be sensitive to the many demands on teachers' time, asking only for assessments that save, rather than waste, time. While we have no time for educational autopsies, we can make time for physicals. Menus can save time for teachers by diverting student energy from endless and meaningless paperwork drills (in which students resubmit work until the teacher is worn out) to a thoughtful and rigorous engagement in demonstrations of student learning. In sum, formative assessment, at the individual, classroom, and school levels, require thoughtful data analysis. Teachers who have experienced dreary meetings labeled as "looking at data" understand the difference between the fear of numbers-based judgment and the promise of constructive data analysis, which is the subject of our next chapter.

CHAPTER 8

Perform Constructive Data Analysis

A hallmark of successful high poverty schools is the ability of teachers and administrators to conduct constructive analysis on the data they collect. In this chapter, we will first discuss the less-effective methods of data analysis that typically involve looking at data for data's sake. These are the situations in which advocates for one point of view or another are on a data safari, hunting the data that will support their pre-established point of view. The impulse to place conclusions before evidence is not the exclusive province of any one viewpoint. Critics of public education focus on evidence of failure and conveniently exclude evidence of success. Critics of charter schools do the same. At the classroom level, I hear people claim that a particular curriculum, assessment, or pedagogical strategy works or doesn't work based on personal experience or the hearsay from a colleague, with little consideration of the reality that what "works" is never a function of a curriculum or practice alone, but rather a function of its effective implementation. Second, we will discuss the educational practices that use data not as a cudgel but as insight. Educational leaders and teachers who adopt these practices protect staff members from those who narrowly examine the data to support their conclusions, and instead use data on both student performance and teaching practices to identify, document, and replicate effective teaching practices.

Looking at Data

As student performance data become more widely available, one of the strangest phenomena in schools is the claim that leaders and teachers are "looking at data" as if they are looking at strange and unfamiliar animals in the zoo. "Look at the data in their habitat!" they seem to be saying. Although it is possible that looking at data is better than avoiding the sight of data, there is not much evidence that the mere observation of data helps student achievement any more than observation of oceans helps prevent climate change effects in Antarctica.

The least helpful manifestation of the "looking at data" trend is the unfortunately named *war room*, a fixture in many educational systems. In these war rooms, one can find charts and graphs detailing the test scores of students for the entire district, broken down subject by subject, school by school. In some systems, these rooms are the settings for intense meetings in which principals and other building administrators are brought in for quarterly confessionals to acknowledge their failings and vow to do better. These public humiliations appear to validate the architects of the war rooms, but otherwise only serve to stimulate endless leader turnover in low-performing schools. The evidence is clear: administrators in low-performing, high-poverty schools are dramatically more likely to leave than leaders in successful schools (Louisiana State University Shreveport, 2018). Likewise, teacher turnover is greatest in schools with the greatest needs (Reeves, 2018). The result is high-poverty schools suffer from turnover and the resulting inconsistency of leadership and teaching. Every new program and practice, however well-intentioned, is hampered from the outset.

Less destructive than war rooms but similarly ineffective are the charts that adorn school board rooms around the globe displaying only student results without a hint as to what caused them. Thus, reading and mathematics scores from a bevy of standardized tests surround school board members as they make decisions about policy and funding. These expensive displays that show "mathematics scores are low" are about as illuminating as those that might indicate "administrators balding" or "legislators overweight." The data may be accurate, but the data displays do little to illuminate how to improve mathematics scores. Although I do not doubt the good intentions of those who insist on displaying data, it is imperative to challenge a process that focuses exclusively on effects. You need not mere data displays, but insight about the data.

Using Data as Insight

Consider two groups of high school mathematics and science teachers, all serving a high-poverty educational system where student failure rates are unacceptably high. Both groups hear the same message, but each group has radically different ways of addressing the concerns. The first group simply lowers its standards and presto! Failing students suddenly have higher grades. These students will, of course, fail their next classes because they are ill-prepared for the next level of instruction, but the group has addressed the immediate concern. When all teachers need to consider is the effects—student scores—then that is all they address.

The second group of teachers takes the more difficult, but far more effective, course of action. Their obligation is not merely to meet the short-term political imperative of improving student scores but to genuinely improve student performance. Therefore, the group begins by determining a consistent measurement of student performance so all students are held to the same standard. Then the group considers changes in teaching practices that will lead to real gains in performance, not merely illusory gains in student scores. This is precisely what I observed teachers in San Bernardino City Unified School District in California do. Their data were not merely about improving student performance—via dramatic reductions in Ds and Fs in core high school mathematics and science classes—but also about improving teaching practices. Most important, their data documented that improvements in student performance were not the result of grade inflation, but rather *work inflation*—students worked harder and earned higher grades.

In 2018, I was privileged to watch Michael Doll, Tom Pham, and Steven Flitch present their findings to every administrator in one of the largest school systems in the United States, San Bernardino City Unified School District. More than 90 percent of the district's students qualify for free or reduced-price lunch, and many students do not speak English at home. In 2009, the high school graduation rate was barely above 60 percent. In 2019, it exceeds 90 percent and continues to increase.

But this is not a decades-long success story. It's about what these three amazing educators did in a single semester. Mr. Doll teaches ninth- and tenth-grade mathematics. Mr. Pham and Mr. Flitch teach high school science. These educators have three things in common.

1. They have high expectations for the academic rigor their students must achieve.

2. They made dramatic changes to their grading practices to focus on student proficiency rather than compliance.

3. They dramatically decreased the failure rate of their students.

Let me anticipate the questions you might have upon reading these commonalities.

1. **That's great for the committed new teachers, but what about the veterans?** All three of these teachers are veterans, with more than twenty years in the classroom. Veterans and new teachers alike are capable of effecting lasting change.

2. **What if my school's union, state or provincial law, or long-term practice won't allow any changes?** This school district did not change contracts and had no authority of state laws. Rather, teachers, union leaders, and administrators all shared a common interest in improving student achievement and reducing failure. All teachers benefited, and continue to benefit, not only from fewer failures but also from the better discipline, classroom climate, and school culture associated with fewer student failures.

3. **What if we can't make any changes without the school board, school, or department making changes?** This district believes in inside-out change using pilot projects and teacher-to-teacher mentoring and support. These leaders don't need to wait for school board, school, or department policies to change to start improvements right now.

4. **What about grade inflation? Doesn't higher performance just reflect an artificial increase in grades without real improvements in student performance?** One of the best things that skeptical mathematics and science teachers bring to the table is a bias toward evidence and hypothesis testing. The concern over grade inflation was precisely their focus when they analyzed three years of final exam scores. If grade inflation was the problem, then one would expect the data to show higher grades but stagnant and lower performance on exams. Instead, the opposite happened; as grades increased, final exam scores also increased. That is not grade inflation, the teachers explained—that's work inflation. Students are working harder, learning more, and thereby achieving higher grades and improved exam scores.

In sum, the key that distinguishes data displays from data insight is data insight depends on causes, not merely effects. Data insight is about teaching and leadership practices, not student test scores.

Summary

Although it is true that high-performing, high-poverty schools, including equity and excellence schools, use student-achievement evidence as a cornerstone of their leadership and teaching decisions, the ways they use data are strikingly different from what I observed in low-performing schools. Most schools, particularly those in high-poverty environments, use data as threats or engage at "looking at data" as if observing animals at a zoo. By contrast, the high-performing schools use data as a source of insight. The critical distinction is, while most schools look only at *effects*—test scores, attendance, discipline, and so on—the most successful schools also consider *causes*—the specific and measurable actions of teachers and school leaders. Whether a student performance is good or bad, the most effective leaders and teachers know the *why* behind the data and take ownership of those results. They know, for example, if their policies about grading, homework, parent communication, absences, and discipline are related to student performance or not. They can test adjustments in professional practices and policies to assess the impact those changes have on student performance. They know, in brief, the difference between *grade inflation* and *work inflation*. They know not only what the student scores reveal but also, and most important, what the data reveal about adult actions.

Insightful data analysis requires professional collaboration among teachers and agreement about student performance and professional practices. When this collaborative ethic is taken to the classroom, teachers must agree on the fundamental building blocks of student performance—the skills, knowledge, and concepts that together form understanding. It is, as Eaker and Keating (2015) suggest, "kid by kid, skill by skill" (p. vi). It is this specific and deliberative level of collaboration we turn our attention to in the next chapter.

CHAPTER 9

Engage in Cross-Disciplinary Units of Instruction

"The Pythagorean theorem? You've got to be kidding! I don't even know if Pythagoras himself found this stuff very interesting. Why do I need to learn it?" Almost every teacher has heard this refrain, or some variation of it, many times. When a teacher responds, "Because it's going to be on the test," his or her persuasive powers stop. The argument that knowledge and skills are useful only if they are tested only serves to reinforce the students' conviction that there is an expiration date on the value of what teachers teach, and that date is approximately one nanosecond after the test is complete! Whether the argument is with a secondary school student about the value of the Pythagorean theorem or a contention with a second grader over the value of persuasive writing, the essence of the discussion is the same: How will students use what we are teaching? The answer lies in a multidisciplinary approach to learning.

In this chapter, we will discuss how equity and excellence schools improve the real-world nature of their students' learning by conducting cross-disciplinary units of instruction. First, we will investigate how cross-disciplinary tasks can enhance engagement in a previously unengaged student population. Second, we will discover the concept of *power standards*, which enable time-strapped teaching staff to devote time and energy to cross-disciplinary work in addition to their regular course load.

Engaging Students With Cross-Disciplinary Tasks

Teachers use persuasive writing, for example, not only because it is one of the genres of composition that might be on the state or provincial test but also because it is an opportunity for students to think more clearly and express empathy for the viewpoints of others. It is a valuable skill in the real world. But if I ask a group of students how valuable persuasive writing is, I might receive some blank stares. In doing the equity and excellence research (Reeves, 2004), I reviewed student writing portfolios and was astonished to find that in the low-performing, high-poverty schools, student writing was overwhelmingly fiction, fantasy, and personal narratives. In equity and excellence schools, by contrast, there was a much richer balance in student writing, with descriptive, persuasive, and analytical writing all playing prominent roles in the literacy curriculum. But—and this is the key for this chapter—the responsibility for writing fell not just on language arts teachers. Students in every class, every grade, and every subject participated in nonfiction writing. The reasons are clear: writing is *thinking*, and every class—art, music, social studies, science, and so on—requires thinking. Therefore, in Elkhart Community Schools in Indiana, the best-performing urban district in the state, students engage in writing in every class, every subject, every grade, every month. At Greenfield Middle School in Greenfield, Wisconsin, teachers created a simplified writing rubric every teacher in every subject can use. In Illinois, the state band championship school has students write a brief paragraph about how they play as individuals and as an ensemble every week. In every class, there are reflection and thinking opportunities writing can enhance.

But writing is only one expression of multidisciplinary instruction. When I was a middle school mathematics teacher in a school with a substantial number of families who had recently arrived in the United States and who spoke little English at home, my students needed to learn about area, perimeter, scale, ratio, and measurement. There are certainly a number of test items I could drill them on so they memorized these isolated bits of knowledge, but instead I asked them to design their ideal school. First, they described the school in words and then drew a picture, not to scale, of their school. Every student, including those with cognitive impairments, would engage enthusiastically in these tasks. Next, students created two-dimensional scale models of their ideal school. While they were focused on the student lounge—an integral part of any ideal school middle school students design—their careful measurements, scale drawings, and determination of the perimeter and area of every room to them seemed incidental. During this two-week performance assessment, some students would finish early and proceed to work beyond the grade-level standard. In this case, that work included a three-dimensional model and the display of their work to architects and engineers in an in-person or virtual setting. This assessment was far from perfect, and I am confident my fellow educators will improve it. But one thing is certain: none of my students asked, "How will I ever use this?" They knew they couldn't design the student lounge in their ideal school if they couldn't master the skills of scale, ratio, area, perimeter, measurement, and all the other seemingly "dumb and irrelevant stuff" that their stodgy old mathematics teacher wanted them to learn.

Teachers rarely know in advance what students will find engaging. The unit on immigration policy and economic impact that caught the imagination of my high school classes (that included large numbers of immigrants) grew stale a few years later. The units on aviation that seemed to entrance middle school mathematics students in the past is less interesting now that air travel is less mysterious and exclusive. Engagement, therefore, is a continuing challenge. But one thing is certain: teachers are more likely to engage students with a multidisciplinary approach than when they focus only on the academic requirements of a single subject.

I can, for example, make mathematics come alive when I can collaborate with my colleagues in science to create mathematical models of biological and chemical processes. I can help students communicate in their persuasive essays in English or make analytical presentations in social studies by integrating a graphical display of information. In equity and excellence schools, sometimes this happens with explicit planning and deliberation, and other times it is more spontaneous. For example, physical education teachers can use measurement, counting, and time problems in their very engaging activities. Music teachers can emphasize fractions as students count and drum out rhythms in halves, fourths, and eighths. Art teachers can help students paint creatively with combinations of geometric shapes. Other examples of multidisciplinary instruction abound and all require school leaders to create the time and space for necessary common planning. For example, in a school where students speak more than thirty languages and with many new arrivals to the English-speaking host country, the art teacher collaborates with the English language arts teachers to create posters with student artwork representing important vocabulary words. These vivid visual images, associated with words in English and several other languages, have those words or phrases printed under the visual image. In another case, an

AP European history teacher uses examples from music and art to help students understand the excesses of Louis XVI that led to the French Revolution.

It is important to note that these teachers had no more time, money, or contractual flexibility than others. Rather, they made a decision to collaborate with colleagues because it made their classes more engaging for both the students and themselves. In some cases, the collaboration was formal, with teachers co-creating an assignment that students could receive credit for in two different classes. For example, students in both literature and history classes receive credit for a literary analysis of their choice of *Uncle Tom's Cabin* (Stowe, 2005), *I Know Why the Caged Bird Sings* (Angelou, 1969), or *Richard II* (Shakespeare, 2016). The English teacher evaluates their understanding of literature and written expression, and the history teacher evaluates their application of characters, plot, and setting to historical and contemporary events. This works well in smaller schools where the same students are likely to share a pair of teachers in English and history. However, in larger schools, or schools without coordinated schedules, this sort of formal coordination is nearly impossible. Nevertheless, I have seen excellent examples of multidisciplinary assessment even in large comprehensive schools where formal coordination ranged from haphazard to nonexistent. For example, in Lee County, Florida, I recall an AP European history teacher who systematically, but informally, integrated music and art into her classes in a school of more than four thousand students (Reeves, 2008a). She engaged in cross-disciplinary instruction not because it was convenient, but because it was necessary, engaging, and fun.

Setting Power Standards for Cross-Disciplinary Instruction

Allow me to engage in a bit of mind reading. Many readers of this book are thinking, "Cross-disciplinary instruction is great, Doug, but I don't have a seven-hundred-day school year. How can I possibly devote a full week or two to a cross-disciplinary classroom activity when I have so many standards to cover?" Their concern is warranted. In California, for example, K–6 teachers have about thirty discrete elements of mathematics alone students need to learn, and the number of standards only increases at the secondary level (California State Board of Education, 2019). Astonishingly, these demands are fewer since the adoption of the Common Core State Standards, as previously established state standards were even more numerous. Although the Common Core standards promised to be "fewer and focused" in comparison, they assume each student only needs to improve by one year of academic growth each year. This assumption is wholly unwarranted in the vast number of schools I have observed, and the assumption is particularly without merit in schools with high concentrations of students living in poverty. To put a fine point on it, it's difficult to teach exponents in seventh grade when students don't know their fourth-grade multiplication tables. It's difficult to teach science and social studies in ninth grade when students are reading at a fifth-grade level. The greatest challenge teachers have is finding time. Although Title I schools often have additional financial resources, money alone is not sufficient to address the needs of teachers and students. They need more time.

There are very isolated experiments, such as those in Massachusetts in 2019, to assess the impact of more instructional time on student results (Massachusetts Department of Elementary and Secondary Education, n.d.). However, for a variety of reasons—after-school sports, care for younger siblings, or jobs necessary to support families, to name a few—many students who most need additional instructional time do not receive it. Therefore, the answer to the dual challenges of too many standards and not enough time to address them is not rapid speech by teachers, but employing *power standards*. Power standards are particularly important in the context of high-poverty schools because teachers encounter many students who arrive at school significantly below grade level. That is, sixth-grade students come to middle school reading on a fourth-grade level; or ninth-grade students arrive in algebra class without the skills in number operations, fractions, and decimals that proficient seventh-grade students should have. As a result, teachers are confronted with the task of addressing two, three, or more grades of curriculum in a single year. Absent a twenty-four-hour school day, they must therefore focus on a few standards. But which standards should be addressed? The answer is *power standards*. Here are their characteristics (Reeves, 2004).

1. **They have leverage:** The standards occur in more than one subject.

2. **They have endurance:** The standards occur year after year.

3. **They are essential:** The standards are required to advance to the next level of study.

Leverage requires a standard be applicable in multiple disciplines. For example, evidence presented previously in this book strongly suggests nonfiction writing has leverage, as proficiency in this core skill is associated with improved student performance in mathematics, science, and social studies. Similarly, the requirement for students to create and draw inferences from tables, charts, and graphs is a requirement not only in mathematics but also in science and social studies. Although it may appear easier to identify standards with leverage, the practical and political challenge comes when educators try to identify standards lacking this quality. Any time we suggest that a standard—say, *manipulating irregular polygons*—is less important than proficiency in tables, charts, and graphs, the advocates for the rhombus and trapezoid come out of the woodwork. I heard one state education official say, "I'll tell you what the power standards are—all of them." This assertion could only originate in the mind of a person who has not been in a classroom for a few decades and for whom frantic coverage of everything seems like a clever strategy.

So, let me be clear about what *is* essential and what *is not*. If administrators ask the English teacher to focus more on nonfiction writing, not just during the month assigned to persuasive writing but throughout the year, then they relieve him or her of the burden of prepositional phrases. If we want the mathematics teacher to focus on number operations, fractions, and decimals, then administrators must say, loud and strong, that the demands of state standards for mastery of the trapezoid, parallelogram, and rhombus are not ultimately helpful to the student who must prepare for the next level of learning.

Standards with leverage are clear from an examination of all standards as well as the research on particular skills that have an impact on many different subjects. For example, the standards that require students to support a claim with evidence are present in many science, social studies, English language arts, and mathematics standards. The evidence cited in chapter 6 (page 55) made clear that nonfiction writing offers leverage—that is, better performance in nonfiction writing is strongly associated with better student performance in science, mathematics, social studies, and reading. It would be great if some external authority, such as the district, state, or intergalactic education federation, would decide what the power standards should be, but that is a vain hope. The reason is that at the state level, standards arise from a process of accumulation. Many constituencies provide input, and if their particular interest is omitted, then the standard-setting authorities are accused of directing their particular point of view. Therefore, the standards promulgated by state authorities are inevitably designed not to narrow the focus of curriculum but to expand it. Even states that have promised standards that were more focused, such as those states that adopted the Common Core State Standards, created standards based on the presumption that students only need one year of learning, an assumption that is rarely true in high-poverty schools.

Endurance is the second criterion for power standards, and however obvious it sounds, many workshops on standards-based instruction ignore this principle. Fourth-grade teachers focus on fourth-grade standards; ninth-grade teachers focus on ninth-grade standards, and so on. But this myopic focus on grade-level standards ignores the principle of endurance. For example, the requirement for argumentative writing recurs in elementary, middle, and high school years. While elementary teachers might find argumentative writing boring and irrelevant, particularly when compared to the student affinity for acrostics and haiku the enduring nature of argumentative writing throughout the K–12 curriculum makes it imperative at every grade level.

The third criterion for power standards is that they are *essential* for the next level of instruction. It is not unusual to see fifth-grade teachers frantically engaged in the coverage of twenty or thirty standards in a single subject such as mathematics, all because "we have to get the students ready for middle school." This is even more challenging for eighth-graders because, teachers explain, "We have to get the students ready for high school." But every time I ask teachers about what is most essential for arriving students to know and be able to do, I always hear a focus on a few essentials. And never—*not once*—have I heard teachers say that the success of arriving students depends on teachers in the previous grade covering every single standard.

Let's consider the example of middle school mathematics. I would nominate the following as power standards for sixth grade.

1. Perform number operations (add, subtract, multiply, and divide) with and without a calculator.

2. Perform fraction and decimal operations.

3. Create tables, charts, and graphs from a data set and draw inferences from them.

4. Create an accurate two-dimensional scale drawing, showing skills in measurement, perimeter, area, scale, and ratio.

5. Given a story problem, write the equation to solve it. Given a formula, create a story problem.

6. Identify the properties of a rectangle and triangle.

That's it. I wish I had time for the rhombus, probability, box plots, the parallelogram, and everything else I left out, but I know my colleagues in the next grade level are far more interested in having students who have these six core skills than in having students who received cursory exposure to the rhombus. These few power standards meet all three criteria. They have leverage; science and social studies standards commonly require skills in operations, measurement, and graphs, for example. They have endurance because they recur in grade after grade. Most important, these skills are essential for the next level of learning. When teachers narrow the focus to power standards, multidisciplinary assessments are much easier to construct, and they have time to devote to deeper and more complex projects and tasks that include subjects outside their direct concern.

Summary

Very young students will sometimes do what we ask in school because the smiles and affirmations of teachers are among their greatest joys. But before too long, the wise third or fourth grader will ask, "When will I ever use this?" By the time students are in middle and high school, it is a question they ask on a daily, perhaps even hourly, basis. They deserve a direct answer, and one that requires some reflection. They don't read Homer, solve equations, or learn about global conflict because facts about these items might be on a future test or so they can drop into conversations with college admissions officers allusions to Scylla and Charybdis, Pythagoras, or Winston Churchill. Students engage in these subjects because they matter. The story of Odysseus allows students to think about resilience in the face of adversity. Understanding mathematics will help them be critical consumers of the claims of marketers, politicians, and, for that matter, teachers. Thinking about Churchill will help them grapple with how commitments to justice and inequality, courage and racism, and leadership and thoughtless classism can all coexist in the same controversial personality. We owe our students engaging work—*work worth doing*. That is far more likely to happen with multidisciplinary tasks in which teachers expand their horizons beyond the exigencies of short-term tests and curriculum coverage.

Teachers will only have time for these sorts of deep reflections, however, when they stop the madness of frantic coverage of scores—even hundreds—of academic standards. The answer is *power standards*, a commitment to mastery of those standards with leverage and endurance and that are most essential for the next level of learning.

The challenge before us now is to transform theory into practice. That is the subject of the next part of this book.

| PART III |

Applying the Research in Your Schools

Parts I and II laid the groundwork for *why* the seven practices in successful high-poverty schools are essential and *why* leaders can have confidence implementing these ideas in every school. In part III, we consider the *how* of the successful practices in high-poverty schools. This is not a cookbook, laying out specific, sequential steps for educators to follow, but rather a system of support that includes the essential mindset for implementing these successful practices, along with a new model of educational change. The key to effective inside-out change is teacher leadership, and we consider examples of how teachers successfully identify challenges, test alternative interventions, and display compelling results. The fundamental premise of these chapters and of the entire book is that equity and excellence are inseparable, and it is meaningless to pursue one without the other.

CHAPTER 10

Discover the Equity and Excellence Mindset

The first step in successfully implementing equity and excellence practices in high-poverty schools is to develop what I call the *equity and excellence mindset*. This chapter begins by introducing the key difference between the equity and excellence mindset and Stanford University professor Carol S. Dweck's (2008) prevailing theory of *fixed* versus *growth* mindset and defining mindset as a *continuum*. This chapter then discusses ways to develop the equity and excellence mindset, including how educators striving to apply equity and excellence practices aim for equity in their thinking and behavior. Finally, we will learn from several case studies that demonstrate the ability to apply the equity and excellence mindset, anytime, anywhere.

Defining Mindset as a Continuum

Dweck (2008) popularizes the term *mindset* by distinguishing between students with a *fixed* mindset and students with a *growth* mindset. Her compelling research suggests students with a *fixed mindset* maintain the belief that ability is fixed at birth and some people will just never overcome a natural lack of talent for mathematics, gymnastics, or writing, no matter how much they might practice. Students with a *growth mindset*, by contrast, seem to know our minds are elastic and skills can improve with practice and diligence. An important element of her conclusion is the conviction that *belief precedes behavior:*

> For twenty years, my research has shown that the view you adopt
> for yourself profoundly affects the way you lead your life. It can
> determine whether you become the person you want to be and
> whether you accomplish the things you value. . . . Believing that
> your qualities are carved in stone—the fixed mindset—creates
> an urgency to prove yourself over and over. If you have only a
> certain amount of intelligence, a certain personality, and a certain
> moral character—well, then you'd better prove that you have a
> healthy dose of them. (Dweck, 2008, p. 6)

The idea that our early predispositions shape our entire lives is hardly a 21st century debate, as Plato, more than two millennia before Dweck, taught that there were men of gold, silver, and bronze. However, in a grudging nod to Dweck's insight, Plato acknowledged that, under the right conditions, the bronze man could become silver, or even potentially gold.

My views on mindset suggest that it is not a dichotomy of fixed versus growth, but rather a continuum. This perspective acknowledges the real world in which equity and excellence teachers, parents, administrators, and students live. If, for example, we were to divide the world into a dichotomy of fixed versus growth mindset, the growth subset would fail to acknowledge the real effects of fetal alcohol syndrome, malnutrition, or poverty and its multiple deprivations. Conversely, the fixed subset would ignore the impact of family members, teachers, technology, and friends who intervene in our lives and provide us with opportunities to grow and flourish in spite of birth circumstances. The reality, of course, is both subsets hold to truths that affect the ways we learn and grow.

We must, therefore, extend our perceptions beyond the limits of fixed and growth mindset and consider instead a *mindset continuum*. The fundamental shift in the scientific evidence since the popularization of fixed and growth mindsets is that, while Dweck (2008) was right in her characterizations of the two mindsets, she was wrong in the sequence; it is not that *belief precedes behavior* but rather that *behavior precedes belief* (DeSteno, 2018; Young, 2017). This new approach values Dweck's original insights but adds an essential element in the context of equity and excellence schools by making clear that behavior precedes belief, a reverse of the sequence Dweck (2008) hypothesized. Research from Hattie (as cited in Waack, n.d.), Donohoo (2017), and EPIC Impact Education Group President and CEO Bobby Moore (2018) makes clear that when teachers have evidence-based convictions, they influence student learning; it becomes a self-fulfilling prophecy. Consider these specific examples:

- Most teachers grew up in an environment in which the bright students—often future teachers—raised their hands to answer questions from the teachers. That made the teacher happy and reaffirmed the bright and eager student. When teachers are encouraged to use *equity sticks*—that is, when they randomly choose students for responses whether or not their hands were raised—the process feels counterintuitive. They fear that they are putting the reluctant students on the spot and that they are ignoring the eager students, the latter being mirror images of themselves. Therefore, few teachers have buy-in to equity sticks or other methods of cold-calling on students. Only when they engage in this practice, however reluctantly, do they then acknowledge higher levels of engagement.

- Many teachers in subjects outside of English language arts are reluctant to require student writing. After all, they have content to deliver, and they were not trained as teachers of writing. Only after, however reluctantly, assigning writing requirements in their classes and observing the results in better thinking, reasoning, and understanding will they decide that writing was a good idea.

In other words, what used to be a fixed mindset about academic achievement and intellectual ability is reversed, not by a workshop about efficacy or a speech about mindset but by *action*—the visible evidence that professional practices of teachers and leaders and the deliberate practice of students leads to improved performance.

Developing an Equity and Excellence Mindset

The equity and excellence mindset represents a fundamental advancement beyond the traditional approach to growth and fixed mindsets. Because behavior precedes belief, we must create a new mindset model that includes, in order, the equity mindset, excellence mindset, and leadership mindset. This is particularly important in high-poverty schools because the terms *equity* and *excellence* have come to mean very different things depending on the context. *Equity* is about equal access to great educational opportunities, but unless those opportunities demand excellence, then equity is a hollow promise. *Excellence* can, depending on the context, mean exceptional performance or a superficial affirmation. In wealthy schools, students are routinely required to rewrite papers, lab reports, and mathematical proofs because the term *excellence* requires comparison to an objective standard of performance. In too many high-poverty schools, by contrast, excellence is not about performance but about affirmation by well-intentioned adults who substitute the words "Great effort!" for "I know you can do better; please do it again." The latter is a risky move, but it is a direct reflection of the real difference in equity. Wealthy students are routinely told to take feedback, do the work again, and improve it. Poor students are more often told that their work is great because it was submitted on time and generally responsive to the directions. In brief, the equity and excellence mindset is not about our attitudes and beliefs but about our professional practices.

We do not start with the premise of the sheriff in the classic movie *Cool Hand Luke* (Carroll & Rosenberg, 1967)—"You got to get your mind right"—but rather, we must get organizational and professional practices right—and then, over time, our mindsets will change.

The Equity Mindset

The equity mindset begins with the premise that every student, regardless of socioeconomic status, ethnic or linguistic identity, or ability or disability, deserves an equal opportunity for a great education. The equity mindset is not about equal results but about equal opportunity, and teachers and leaders with the equity mindset are vigilant about potential barriers to equal opportunity. For example, if one element of equity is the opportunity to take college-level classes in high school, a barrier would be the fact the poor students might be diverted from those opportunities because of decisions made in elementary and middle school. The equity mindset would require schools to redirect those students toward college opportunities, even if students and parents thought that those opportunities had been denied to them. Thus, the equity mindset is about identifying barriers and removing them, providing opportunity for every student at every level of education.

This explanation of the equity mindset suggests educators need to take the concepts of a growth mindset and put them into action. The evidence of an equity mindset is not based on rhetoric, but on actual leadership and teaching behaviors. For example, one manifestation of the equity mindset is the way schools identify, recruit, and assign students to advanced courses. In many school systems, students of color are less likely to be guided into advanced courses and are often unlikely to seek those courses themselves. For example, I have seen schools create the illusion of equity by increasing enrollment in college-level classes, but when it comes time to take the external examinations that might validate the work of these students for college credit, few students from low-income families take or pass the exams. Thus, we have the honor roll illusion, in which students achieve honor roll grades, then apply for and are accepted into college, go deeply into debt, and soon flunk out of college because equity was, for them, an illusion and not a reality. This is not necessarily the result of overt bias, but rather of circular reasoning; students who are economically disadvantaged are often considered educationally disadvantaged, receiving less rigorous preparation and expectations in their early schooling years. These differences start at a very early age and, a decade later, lead to the self-fulling prophecy—these students are unprepared for advanced courses. Authors Stacey M. Childress, Denis P. Doyle, and David A. Thomas (2009) conclude that by the time they are third and fourth graders, low-income minority students are, on average, nearly three grade levels behind in reading and mathematics, and the vast majority never catch up. This influences the views of students, teachers, and counselors.

The equity mindset requires leaders to scrutinize decisions having an adverse impact on selection. When leaders settle for a mindset based on previous test scores rather than an equity mindset, the cycle of disadvantage is endlessly repeated. The conditions that initially led to poverty and low academic performance tend to keep students in poverty and low academic performance. What is essential is for leaders to interrupt the system by identifying crucial decision points that perpetuate academic underperformance.

An analysis of Boston Public Schools reveals systemic inequities that segregate students into high- and low-quality schools, purportedly according to academic merit, but undeniably also according to economic status and ethnic identity (Hamilton, 2018). The quality of the high school is strongly related to the students' ability to complete high school and have the opportunities associated with a high-quality secondary education, so it is important for all students to have an equitable opportunity to attend high-quality schools. However, although Boston boasts some of the best public and private schools in the United States and their leaders would certainly claim to have an equity mindset, the availability of educational quality is based on student access to rigorous preparation they either have or don't have early in life.

One trend in many educational organizations is to designate a *chief equity officer* to work alongside the chief academic officer. However well-intentioned this might be, it sends the message that the system's commitment to equity is somehow different from its commitment to academic excellence. This leads to workshops, initiatives, and programs that appear to focus on equity, but that compete for time and resources focused on academic support. I would make the argument that your district already has a chief equity officer, and that is the superintendent. This is the person committed to the inseparable goals of equity and excellence. This is the person who represents the fundamental notion that any equity program not part of a commitment to academic excellence is ephemeral, and any academic program without an integral commitment to equity is valueless.

Educational systems demonstrate their commitment to equity and excellence not with job titles, but with actions. Systemwide initiatives always include both equity and excellence and do not treat them separately. For example, rather than talking about the concepts of implicit and explicit bias, leaders in equity and excellence schools focus on the evidence. "Here are three samples of fourth-grade student writing," they begin, and then ask, "What do you notice about the similarities and differences in these samples?" What is telling about the equity and excellence mindset is that this examination of student work was not notable or unique to a single school or grade level. It is part of the organizational culture, just the way they do business. This simple exercise—looking at authentic student work—reflects what the school system believes about equity more than any poster, slogan, or workshop on the subject. Most important, these simple but profound exercises lead to actions. Principals and teachers could say, "This, right here, is what fourth-grade students in our schools can and must do, and we cannot accept anything less."

In the most challenging urban systems in the United States, the presence or absence of the equity and excellence mindset is soon evident. Students in the same grade with the same demographics often exhibit strikingly different levels of writing. The original equity and excellence research was based on comparing students, teachers, leaders, and schools that all faced the challenge of more than 90 percent of students coming from low-income families (Reeves, 2004). Sustaining the equity and excellence mindset requires teachers and leaders to view demographic variables as a surmountable factor on the road to high achievement.

The Excellence Mindset

The excellence mindset is based on this provocative question: What would we do if these students were rich? In a New England prep school, where parents routinely pay tuition in excess of $50,000 per year in 2019, there are students who excel and those who struggle. Whether the context is field hockey, lacrosse, algebra, or English literature, there is a consistent mindset of excellence. When a student flubs a goal, fails to balance an equation, or misreads the central message of a poem or novel, the answer is never, "Sink or swim, kid—you should have had that before you got here!" Rather, the message is, and I confess to using some dramatic license here, "This kid is not proficient [in field hockey, algebra, or reading], so what are we going to do about it? After all, their parents are paying fifty grand in tuition, and we'd better make sure they are successful because, after all, that's what rich kids deserve." Let me be clear that I know of many New England prep school leaders and teachers who are deeply committed to equity, but the data do not lie—they have 100 percent graduation rates and sky-high acceptance rates to the world's most elite colleges and universities. Contrast this to the mediocrity mindset in which students are assessed, in Dweck's (2008) terms, at a fixed level of performance from the moment they walk in the door. Poor readers are just poor readers. Poor goal-tenders, mathematicians, and writers are all consigned to the same scrap heap of mediocrity. The excellence mindset is consistent and clear—the response to error and failure is feedback and more work, not a label and ignominy.

The Leadership Mindset

Among the many gifts in my life has been the ability to work with great leaders who challenged me to work beyond what I thought I could do. They did this not because I had any talent or ability but because they knew it was their mission to develop and challenge their colleagues. Mr. Robinson did not ask me about the theory of teaching mathematics but rather adjourned our interview and said, "Let's go to Room 103 and teach a class." From this and many other examples, I learned that the leadership mindset is not about a sophisticated analysis of the capabilities of subordinates but rather about the positive assumption that people will rise to expectations, just as we expect students to rise to our expectations.

The leadership mindset is less concerned with what teachers learned or didn't learn in the process of their teacher preparation programs than with how they respond to challenges in the present movement. Leaders with this mindset do not pretend to have the answers but routinely encourage collaboration and inquiry. The examples earlier in this book about inside-out change (see chapter 8, page 75) could never have occurred without leaders who were willing to trust their colleagues to experiment, make mistakes, learn from these mistakes, and then share their successes and failures with colleagues. They accomplished more in a semester than they would have in one of the many five-year plans that characterize strategic plans around the world.

Applying the Equity and Excellence Mindset, Anytime, Anywhere

The equity and excellence mindset encourages without being patronizing. It offers feedback without being devastating. And the commitment to excellence this mindset represents has nothing to do with a student's economic status or ethnic identity.

The equity and excellence mindset offers a vision for the future. There are educators and leaders, and I have seen them in schools around the world. Science teacher Tom Pham changed the consequences for missing work from failure to incessant demands that students complete the work. Michael Doll deals with more than two hundred mathematics students every day, many of whom would fail his class and, ultimately, drop out of school. No pushover, Mr. Doll demands great work while moving every one of his students across the finish line. Steven Flitch, a skeptical veteran of more than twenty years in his science classroom, demonstrates every day that poverty is not an impediment to achieving at the highest levels—even in the most demanding high school classes.

These educators are clear-eyed, honest, and realistic. They are completely authentic, and their examples demonstrate that equity and excellence mindsets and practices need not be exceptional and can be applied anywhere.

Summary

Dweck (2008) showed the world the power of fixed and growth mindsets. Her work deserves serious consideration by every teacher, parent, and student. But contemporary research takes us beyond the simple dichotomy of a fixed or a growth mindset and the premise that we must change minds before we change actions, policies, and leadership decisions.

This chapter offers a better idea—the equity and excellence leader and educator. Perhaps these practitioners do not have a perfectly implemented growth mindset. They have their frustrations and wishes for better impulses and behaviors. But they have the courage to take action—to implement the successful practices described in part II (page 29) of this book—and from that action and the positive results that follow, an equity and excellence mindset emerges, offering a vision for the future that allows any student, anywhere, to succeed.

We now turn our attention to a new model of educational change—one that depends not on rhetorical devices but on behavior and evidence. The goal is not mystical belief but rational consideration of evidence. And from that evidence, action follows to help students succeed.

CHAPTER 11

Change Behavior Before Belief

One of the biggest challenges in implementing equity and excellence techniques in your school is the inevitable resistance that accompanies any change initiative. Change of any sort represents a loss and is consequently often difficult and painful. It is important to acknowledge the challenges and difficulties associated with change and respect the feelings of colleagues when they are resistant to change. However, equity and excellence schools provide a model for how to successfully implement change. In this chapter, we will begin by discussing the difficulties of change and why it is particularly difficult in systems with high poverty. We will discuss traditional models for change and why they fail. Finally, we will present some techniques for how to manage change to bring about successful and rapid changes desperately needed in high-poverty schools.

Anticipating Resistance and Other Difficulties of Change

Change is hard because it represents loss—loss of previous practice and convictions and, most of all, loss of previous identity. For example, I hope my students turn to me when they need answers, and I hope to be the trusted colleague my peers turn to when facing their most difficult students. So, I am understandably threatened regarding my personal and professional identity as a subject-matter expert when my expertise is on a YouTube video that is more readily accessible than my office hours. When I have objective success—the evidence of which is happy students; heartfelt letters from alumni and parents; and high test scores from Advanced Placement, International Baccalaureate, or other college credit classes—I am not terribly interested to know about alternative styles of pedagogy, assessment, and grading that might better serve my students' interests. I am already successful, so any suggestion to improve is an implication that my success is invalid and illusory. Resistance to change is not a character defect. It is a reflection of the human condition that finds comfort and affirmation in previous practice. The central challenge for change leadership is to distinguish *bad practice* from the *motivation behind bad practice*.

Adam Grant (2019), a professor at the Wharton School at the University of Pennsylvania specializing in organizational psychology, reminds us that cultural change is painful and uncomfortable. Often, the weight-loss industry entices people not because it leads to weight loss, but because it promises pain-free change. Why endure sweat and deprivation when a pill or procedure will do? The same seductions can also occur in schools, as vendors lead decision makers to conclude that after-school programs, technology solutions, or other interventions can save underperforming students without inconvenient and uncomfortable actions requiring changes in schedule, restrictions on time, confrontations with parents, or otherwise difficult and uncomfortable decisions. But just as miracle weight-loss drugs or products are rarely effective, neither are change initiatives without some degree of hard work, discomfort, and yes, pain, as we say farewell to old and comfortable methods.

Even in school systems reporting high achievement, change can be difficult and painful. Chip Kimball, former superintendent of Singapore American School, the largest international school in the world, is globally respected as an innovative leader who took a great school and made it even greater with creative advances in curriculum, assessment, teaching, and leadership. The objective evidence for Kimball's school suggests he advocated highly effective and successful changes, including dramatic expansion of high-level classes, including Singapore's innovative Advanced Topics courses that were designed by teachers to provide deep inquiry into complex subjects. In addition, Singapore pioneered the Catalyst program, in which high school students could get off the academic treadmill and focus on a single area of deep inquiry for two months so that they could pursue a passion and, sometimes, decide that what they thought was a passion was just not that interesting. Either result was positive. Although these changes represented world-class innovation, they were—like all changes—not universally popular. Traditional Advanced Placement classes, for example, offer a greater comfort zone than innovative Advanced Topics classes. Getting off the treadmill for two months to purify water in Cambodia, write a poem, compose a sonata, or build an experiment destined for the International Space Station is contrary to the expectations that many parents have of an eight-period day and homework until midnight as the path to success. Resistance to change is simply a fact of organizational life.

Understanding Change Within Challenging Systems

Although resistance to change exists within any organization, change is supremely difficult for educators in high-poverty schools. These educators may even be *more* resistant to change because their students seem to face disproportionately more challenges than students from less-impoverished backgrounds. While well-off students may face the typical challenges of childhood and adolescence (such as friendship or relationship difficulties, the struggles of maintaining a school-life balance, and anxiety over achieving admission to a desired college or apprenticeship), some students from high-poverty backgrounds come to class in the morning from homeless shelters. They have classmates who have been murdered. They have classmates whose parents are in jail or have been killed by gang violence. They are hungry. They are abused. These students are not interested in strategies for higher test scores; their focus is on survival. Therefore, to suggest teachers of these students improve their practice can be perceived as a slap in the face. These teachers and administrators listen to solutions about improved achievement and think, "You have no idea about the lives of my students. How can any of these programs possibly make a difference in their lives?"

And yet there are, in the midst of these schools, teachers and administrators who simultaneously focus on survival and success, who recognize their students face personal trials and annual tests, and who know there is a world beyond the neighborhoods these students emerge from every day. When I interview students from Newark, New Jersey, to San Bernardino, California, in schools overwhelmed by poverty and social ills, they have a common refrain: "We are safe here." Their teachers call them *scholars*, and they are, if only for a few hours a day, far removed from the factors that threaten them and their future. These teachers prove it is indeed possible for students facing the unthinkable challenges of poverty to still find success in the academic arena.

Indeed, one of the strangest findings from equity and excellence research is the existence of parallel practices between high-poverty schools and some of the highest-performing schools in the world. What do the best schools in Singapore; Newark, New Jersey; Cambridge, Massachusetts; San Bernardino, California; and Newtown and New Haven, Connecticut, have in common? They certainly do not have the same commercial programs or budgets—in fact, the high-poverty schools in these comparisons often have more per-pupil funding than the richer systems. But what they have in common is a set of immutable professional practices. They write. They collaboratively score student work. They showcase great student work. It is this sort of inside-out change that allows these schools to implement and sustain change. In brief, equity and excellence culture is not about posters on the wall or espoused values. Rather, culture is reflected in lived values in objectively observable behaviors. Their cultures reflect not merely the rhetoric of leaders but also the actions of students, teachers, and administrators throughout the system. Consider a couple of examples of how culture is transformed into practice:

- Mr. Wingo, the social studies department chair of a large comprehensive high school, and his colleague, Ms. Bakalar, the English department chair, convene their meetings precisely on time at 2:00 p.m., on the regular early dismissal day for teacher collaboration. They say, almost in unison, "I know that you are all working incredibly hard to create multidisciplinary assessments, but you just have not had the time to finish the job. So, we have agreed to give you the next ninety minutes to work with a colleague in the other department, create a four-task performance assessment that considers academic standards in both English and social studies, and share with us next week." At 2:01 p.m. the meeting is adjourned, and teachers collaborate. It is the most productive department meeting they can recall. While most meetings have traditionally been characterized by one-way communication, teachers were empowered to produce real work not as a homework assignment, but during scheduled work time.

- Dr. Burks is the elementary school principal in a school that includes low-income families, homeless families, and recent immigrant arrivals with children who, due to violence in their home country, have not been in school for several years. She asks her superintendent, "Do we really have to have a staff meeting?" Upon hearing a negative response, Dr. Burks ends scheduled staff meetings with her cultural imperative of equity and excellence and gives that time to teachers to connect with families and students.

With evidence that even the most downtrodden schools are capable of implementing equity and excellence techniques (see part II, page 29), why do other schools fail? The answer is that despite a tsunami of books, articles, and speeches on the subject of change, there are fundamental flaws in many prevailing change theories to consider in order to take the equity and excellence strategies (see part I, page 7) and move them from theory into practice.

Prevailing Change Theory

Harvard Business School professor John P. Kotter (1996, 2012) has been the leading exponent of change leadership since the 1980s. Fullan (2008, 2016) did the same for the field of education. Since the 1980s, these scholars have been the most influential theorists on the foundations of organizational change. Although he began with a business perspective, schools widely adopted and the American Association of School Administrators promoted Kotter's (2009, 2012) change leadership theories. Kotter (2012) suggests the following eight-stage change process.

1. Establish a sense of urgency.

2. Create a guiding coalition.

3. Develop a vision and strategy.

4. Communicate the change vision.

5. Empower employees for broad-based action.

6. Generate short-term wins.

7. Consolidate gains and produce more change.

8. Anchor new approaches in the culture.

Despite the wide adoption of Kotter's (1996, 2012) change model, he concludes that the vast majority of change efforts fail. One explanation is, despite the time and resources schools devote to this change model, the implementation is simply insufficient. Perhaps, Kotter (2012) suggests, the guiding coalition is not powerful enough or the people in charge allow too much complacency. But there is another explanation—the model itself is wrong. The model assumes urgency, and the change that follows is based on organizational leadership effectively communicating the need for change.

From the 1960s to the early 2000s, the findings on resistance to change have been remarkably similar: facts don't change people's minds (Varol, 2017). Making a compelling case for change certainly seems reasonable, but it is fundamentally insufficient to make individuals and organizations engage in meaningful change. Few school leaders and educators receive the change-or-die message, although the consequences of educational failure can be dire for students (see, for example, All4ed.org). If people will not change when the alternative is dying a painful death and missing experiences with those they love, then why would anyone expect that creating a sense of urgency for educational systems, corporations, or nonprofit organizations is going to lead to change? There is a prevailing mythology of change leadership: if we just find the right blend of persuasion, research, and emotional appeal, then staff will embrace the changes leaders wish to make. This false belief is based on the myth of *buy-in*—that is, in order to implement effective change, leaders must first gain widespread staff agreement. When leaders tell me they have buy-in from all staff members, one of two things is true: (1) they are not really asking for significant changes or, more likely, (2) the real resistance is happening underground, out of the leader's earshot. This is why the vast majority of change, initiatives fail. Kotter (2012) estimates more than 90 percent of change efforts are not implemented as intended.

I am not suggesting leaders bully and intimidate subordinates into change. Rather, leaders must change the conversation from a desperate appeal for agreement to a thoughtful, respectful, and reasoned approach to the uncertainty and difficulty surrounding all change efforts. As Alan Deutschman (2007) finds, change *is* possible, whether it is reducing heart disease through altered lifestyles, reducing prison recidivism, or making other dramatic social, individual, and organizational changes. However, those most effective changes don't happen with the rhetoric of urgency. Rather, change happens because behavior precedes belief, the central lesson of cognitive psychology we consider in the next section.

Learning From Cognitive Psychology

Those implementing organizational change can learn much from the field of cognitive psychology. In particular, there is overwhelming evidence about cognitive behavioral therapy (CBT) showing changes in thought processes that have as great or greater impact on patient outcomes as pharmaceuticals, such as Prozac (Burns, 1980; Gillihan, 2018). CBT is based on identifying six fundamental errors in thinking and having patients learn to identify and counteract these errors in thought and perception. This therapeutic approach has significant applications to organizational change as well.

Psychiatrist David D. Burns (1980) categorizes thinking errors in the following ways.

1. All-or-nothing thinking

2. Overgeneralizing

3. Catastrophizing

4. Dismissing the positive

5. Fortune telling

6. Mind reading

If I could synthesize the work of Burns (1980) and his predecessors over the past half-century to the 21st century, it would be in this simple statement: *behavior precedes belief.* For the isolated and fearful person who dreads social interaction, the answer is not the thirty-year plan of therapy sessions about fears of crowds but rather going into small groups, and then larger groups, to engage with the world. Behavior precedes belief.

For the addict and alcoholic, the answer is not waiting for a mindshift that suddenly permits the discovery that drugs and alcohol are not great substitutes for happiness but rather engaging in societal interactions with water rather than alcohol. We fear societal interaction without alcohol-fueled sociability, but we engage in social interactions anyway.

For the teacher who has experienced twenty-five years of parental antagonism and student misbehavior, he or she enters the school door convinced that this day will be like the preceding years, but instead he or she has rearranged the desks and chairs to ensure that there is no longer a back row where students can check out. Each class begins with unexpectedly positive interactions and skeptical students. The new policy of calling on every student randomly creates an environment that is both exciting and scary because every student might be engaged at any time. Not certain that this will really work, the teacher persists.

For the administrator who has become accustomed to dreadful staff meetings in which a few cynics hold up newspapers and visibly check out, and others study their cell phones, he or she announces, "Meeting adjourned," before the antagonistic behavior can start. All the grandstanding, defensiveness, and antagonism that has traditionally dominated the meeting is now gone, and the leader can focus on getting key goals accomplished rather than engaging in another futile meeting.

In all of these examples, there was no buy-in, no belief—just a willingness to try something new and observe the results. The ethic of "we've always done it that way" was replaced with "try it, test it, improve it"—that is, behavior precedes belief.

All-or-Nothing Thinking

I encounter *all-or-nothing thinking* frequently when indicating what interventions evidence suggests will remarkably reduce student failure. For example, schools have widely replicated the *Ketchup Solution*, resulting in reductions of failures by more than 96 percent (Reeves, 2012). In the past, whenever students had missing work, they simply accumulated failing marks until the end of the semester, resulting in hundreds of course failures. When the Ketchup Solution was started, students had only between Monday and Thursday to get work finished. If it was not completed by the end of Thursday, on Friday morning, they were required to report to the Ketchup room, where they would catch up on the week's work. In the original case, a school of approximately 1,200 students went from 138 to five course failures in a single year, all while maintaining the same high academic standards. Teachers simply recognized that, especially in many homes facing the challenges of poverty, homework was not high on the priority list when students had jobs, childcare, and survival occupying most of their attention. When these courageous teachers provided alternative ways to get work done—the Ketchup Solution—failures declined (Reeves, 2012).

Resistance to this solution includes the sentiment, "But I know a student that won't work for." That is true—even in the successful case, five students still failed. But those failures hardly diminish the importance of the overall dramatic improvement. All-or-nothing thinking, however, leads people to conclude if a solution is not perfect and does not work for all students, then it is not worth adopting.

In the context of CBT, some critics would object that the reduction in failures, from 138 to five, only validated their complaint that "I know kids that are defiant, and this will never work for them." That is classic all-or-nothing thinking. The fact that five students did not pass the class is insufficient evidence to undermine the fact that there was a dramatic reduction in failures and suspensions. Perfection is not the standard; improvement is.

Overgeneralizing

An example of *overgeneralizing* occurs when educators inquire into the causes of student failure. Teachers in high-poverty schools frequently face challenges of chronic absenteeism and student misbehavior. These cases can become magnified in importance because they occupy a great deal of the attention of administrators and teachers. Therefore, when I ask, "What is the principal cause of failure?" the answer is frequently about absenteeism and discipline. But a quick look at the gradebooks reveals a starkly different picture. The most common cause for failure is neither absences nor misbehavior, but *missing work*. By overgeneralizing the causes of failure for a few students to the entire student population, we neglect a systematic examination of the evidence that might lead to a solution.

I have often asked teachers and administrators to tell me the most common cause of student failures. The most frequent response is that student attendance is poor. That is certainly a valid concern, but it does not bear up under scrutiny. In data that I have analyzed but not yet published, the ratio of student failure due to missing assignments compared to student failure due to poor attendance, based on an examination of report cards and teachers' comments, was twenty to one—that is, for every student who failed due to poor attendance, twenty failed due to missing work. Although there is no doubt that some students fail due to poor attendance, it is an overgeneralization to say that the primary cause of failure is poor attendance.

Catastrophizing

The unfortunate thought process of *catastrophizing* attacks the beleaguered teacher who, seeing disappointing student results, goes down the spiraling thought path from "My students' mathematics scores are low" to "I'm just a terrible teacher, the system is rigged against poor students, the tests are worthless, and I should never have entered this profession in the first place!" There are many causes for low mathematics scores, including poor prior knowledge, misalignment of the curriculum and assessments, and insufficient time for teachers to provide the skills and conceptual knowledge students need for success. Catastrophizing leads to an emotionally toxic environment and, worst of all, increased turnover of teachers and administrators in schools most in need of instructional and leadership stability.

The antidote to catastrophizing is not the abdication of responsibility for students (in other words, "It's not my fault—they should have been better prepared before they came here"). A better cognitive restructuring of this challenge is what I have described as the *three-column challenge*. In this method, we consider every cause for low student performance or, for that matter, low performance in the school, district, and nation. These causes can be divided into three categories:

1. Factors I can control
2. Factors I can influence
3. Factors I cannot control or influence

The key to avoiding catastrophic thinking, along with many other cognitive errors, is to focus on the first two categories—factors we can control and factors we can influence. When teachers, leaders, and students are stuck in the mire of factors they cannot control or influence, then catastrophic thinking inevitably follows.

Dismissing the Positive

Consider the student who writes a beautiful five-paragraph essay. She has a great topic sentence, clear supporting evidence, and beautiful transitions. Her vocabulary is strong—well beyond her grade level—and her conclusion neatly draws the entire piece together. Her report to her parents, however, is, "The teacher hated my second piece of evidence to support my thesis."

Consider the teacher who is no less than brilliant and throughout the year has received great feedback from eight observations by a team of three administrators and colleagues. In one case, one of the observers noted that two boys in the back of the room had their heads down on the tables with earphones on. Although this was clearly an aberration, the teacher's reaction, based on one of twenty-four observations, is that "I have terrible engagement strategies."

Dismissing the positive happens frequently with personnel evaluations. Teachers and administrators may receive positive feedback on thirty areas of professional competence and a need for improvement on two, but it is those two the recipients of the evaluation concentrate on the most. This is one reason so few teachers receive constructive evaluations—it's just not worth the stress of providing accurate feedback on needed improvements (Marshall, 2009). Boards of education also fall victim to this error, looking only at the complaints of a few constituents and discussing the broad satisfaction parents and voters have with public schools. A Gallup poll consistently finds that while the public is concerned with public schools in general, they are consistently satisfied with their own schools (as cited in Phi Delta Kappa International, 2018).

Fortune Telling

Two teachers, Susan and Margaret, walk into the same school at the same time. "This is going to be a great day!" says Susan as she walks into school, warmly greeting students who hug her and who are happy to join her for breakfast in her classroom. Susan thinks, "I was meant to do this, and someday these kids will be parents and thank me for all that I did for them."

"Here we go again," says Margaret, entering the same school with the same students. She notices the curse word from the eighth graders in the corner who are laughing at a wildly inappropriate YouTube video. The trash around the cafeteria after breakfast is horrendous. "Were these kids raised by wolves?" she thinks. As she makes it to her classroom, head down and avoiding eye contact, she overhears students cursing once again. "This is going to be a terrible day," Margaret thinks. "I can't wait for the year to end so that I can do something much more meaningful. I'd rather garden because even the weeds are not so disruptive and rude."

Neither Susan nor Margaret has powers of extrasensory perception. They are not fortune-tellers. Yet both appear to have convinced themselves that they can foretell the future of each day and, indeed, the rest of their lives.

While these two vignettes may be only slightly exaggerated, *fortune telling* plays out in many other ways throughout the school day. One of the most common cases of fortune telling in schools is the pervasive myth, *If the assignment doesn't count, and if teachers don't grade the work, then students won't do it.* Although this idea has intuitive appeal, the evidence does not support it. Thomas R. Guskey (2015), professor of educational psychology in the College of Education at the University of Kentucky, finds when students receive timely and accurate feedback (even without a grade), they perform better than when they receive a grade on their work. It is easy to quell fortune telling with simple experiments and pilot projects. However popular these contentions are, it is better to view them as hypotheses to test.

Mind Reading

Mind reading is the presumption of insight without evidence. For example, as I crossed the street this morning, a black SUV ran a red light, and my insight was that the driver was a drug dealer on the way to a sale, or possibly a distracted teenage driver who will someday die behind the wheel due to reckless driving. It might even have been a preoccupied mother with toddlers in the back seat, who should have been paying better attention. So many minds to read, and so little time.

In the cognitive error of mind reading, the greatest distortion, and the most difficult one to admit, is that we might be wrong. Since Socrates was handed hemlock for corrupting the youth of Athens in 399 BC, school observers have sought to read the minds of adolescents. In some schools, beliefs about student motivation defer more to folklore and personal beliefs than solid science, but that is not due to a lack of available evidence. Rather, it is due to a human predilection for mind reading over evidence.

The same mind reading errors that occur to me on the streets of Boston happen in classrooms every day. "That kid is lazy," I conclude because of missing homework. It's possible that the student is homeless and, as I later discover, slept on a bench in a shopping mall the previous night as his mother cleaned the place. It was a miracle that he even showed up to school at all, and certainly neither he nor his mother is lazy. Likewise, teacher observers may conclude, "That teacher is completely failing to engage her class," not realizing that a student has become ill and then run out the door, rightly occupying the teacher's attention as she trusts her classroom norms to prevail with the remaining students.

Whenever we find ourselves mind reading, an appropriate question to consider might be, Is there at least one other plausible explanation for what I am seeing? If we can find just a single response to that probing question, then our impulse to mind reading might be subject to challenge.

Applying the Lessons of CBT

If educators are to embrace the promise of applying the lessons of cognitive psychology to school change, then they must reject traditional change models, which are based on a presumption of the following sequence of behavioral change.

1. Provide information—usually in the form of workshops, keynote speeches, book studies, and so on.

2. Gain buy-in.

3. Change practice.

4. Observe improved results.

If this sequence represents actual change efforts, then we cannot reconcile Kotter's (1995) own findings that more than 70 percent of change efforts fail and only about 10 percent are implemented as designed. In fact, the lessons of CBT follow a sequence of change behaviors that is quite different.

1. Change practice—even before gaining buy-in.

2. Observe improved results.

3. Gather information on the relationship between practice and results.

4. Gain buy-in.

The central premise of this model is that *behavior precedes belief.* In the recovery community, this is called the *as-if principle.* We act *as if* we are in great physical shape, even as we begin an inconvenient and painful exercise program. We act *as if* we are careful about our diet, alcohol, and drug use, even as we begin a commitment to sobriety. We act *as if* nonfiction writing is an effective strategy, even as doubts plague us because not everyone is persuaded this practice will be effective. Whether the challenge is overcoming a fear of spiders and dogs or speaking to a partner or colleague, CBT's process of desensitization is proven effective. When the challenges are stress, anxiety, and depression, CBT helps medical patients challenge erroneous thought patterns, not by the therapist arguing with the patient, giving a speech to the patient, or providing a daylong workshop. Rather, the patient is equipped with specific tools to challenge errors in his or her thinking, and the patient—not the therapist—can evaluate, challenge, and reframe.

This is precisely the CBT principle that leads to short-term change. Rather than years of Freudian analysis, CBT research provides documented improvements in patients to address severe anxiety, stress, and depression within eight to twelve weeks (Gillihan, 2018). Contrast those results to the claim that change requires five to seven years; it is simply not the case (Fullan & Pinchot, 2018). Organizational change can happen with remarkable speed, just as it does for individuals (Reeves & Eaker, 2019).

Presenting a New Model of Educational Change

Improving change leadership essential to implement and sustain equity and excellence practices requires focus on four fundamental elements: (1) buy-in, (2) coalition building, (3) strategic planning, and (4) sustainability.

The first element of the new change model is to reject the tendency to appeal for buy-in and to instead acknowledge that behavior precedes belief. This is an evidence-based approach: do it, observe the results, gather information, and then—and only then—encourage buy-in. The old model relies on superficial submission. The new model embraces genuine critical thinking and skepticism, which educators resolve with evidence, not rhetoric.

The second element in the new change model is the leader's use of a coalition. Traditionally, the leader builds a coalition often broadly representative of different interest groups. In their pursuit of consensus and inclusiveness, however, these groups can become paralyzing influences on a system, delaying change or even stopping it in its tracks. When each group can throw down the gauntlet, saying, "The board won't do X" or "The union won't do Y" or "The parents' association won't agree to Z," then the system is left with the illusion that the status quo is universally agreeable to everyone. But that is almost never the case—after all, there was a reason for the change initiative in the first place! Rather, everyone wants change, as long as other elements of the system make the changes. For example, almost every teacher I encounter wants students to read more carefully and write more clearly. But if the potential solution stands to be writing in every subject and every grade, their enthusiasm is considerably diminished. When the coalition adopts a focus on mediation among competing interest groups, coalition members can lose sight of the main goal—making dramatic student achievement gains. Students are never members of the coalition, but they nevertheless depend on the adults participating in those meetings to make life-saving decisions. The key to effective change is not the model of Athenian democracy in which every voice is present and there is no connection between volume (that is, the noise that they produce) and volume (the number of people that they represent). Rather, the coalition must be focused on a vision not of the popular present, but a visionary future. After all, if the criterion for effective change is how popular it will be with people whose interests might be disrupted by change, then forget about initiating any change efforts at all.

Third, traditional change efforts involve strategic planning, specifically, the setting of goals for five, seven, or ten years into the future. These plans almost all include an overwhelming number of objectives and initiatives, and fuzzy mission and vision statements that can be mind-numbingly obscure. There are happy exceptions, such as the *Plan on a Page* (Reeves, 2009b, appendix A), but more frequently these plans are cumbersome, time-consuming, and more focused on document production than results. Those who must implement these plans need a clearly focused set of objectives in which actions are linked to results, and those results must be timely. As Robert Eaker and I (2019) argue in *100-Day Leaders*, the key to long-term success is a commitment to short-term results. That is, in order to maintain the confidence and persistence required in any organization to accomplish lasting change, leaders must first establish some short-term wins. Within a single semester, student achievement, discipline, and teacher morale can improve. Within the context of five-year objectives, by contrast, the people who created a change initiative may not be there to see the change to its conclusion.

Fourth, the new model of change is dramatically accelerated, leading to greater sustainability. Even when traditional change theorists acknowledge the need for *short-term wins*, their use of the term is generally associated with gains in one or two years. Leaders can implement very significant changes within one hundred days (Reeves & Eaker, 2019); this is the only way to sustain momentum and validate risks inherent in change leadership. When there are mistakes, the one-hundred-day cycle can fix them immediately. When there are successes, the one-hundred-day cycle provides a flywheel of success, with each success leading to the next, building confidence and competence throughout the system.

This emphasis on one-hundred-day wins is also reflective of the information most important for systemwide change. The Gas Foundation reports that when a very important statistic is reported to an audience, just 5 percent recall it (as cited in Grant, 2019). When reporting about a compelling story, vivid in detail and full of emotional content, more than 60 percent of the audience recall it (as cited in Grant, 2019). Data and evidence are important—but so is the essential human component—*the story behind the numbers.* Perhaps most important, the new change model recuses strategic planners from strategic planning. Researchers Russell Eisenstat, Bert Spector, and Michael Beer (1990) find that, after a four-year study of organizational change, the greatest obstacle to revitalization is the idea that it comes about through companywide change programs, particularly when a corporate staff group such as human resources sponsors them, a phenomenon the researchers call the fallacy of programmatic change.

Let's consider what the new educational change model looks like in practice. In order to reflect the concept that *behavior precedes belief,* there should be no more earnest appeals, inspirational speeches, and imperious demands. Instead, politely request a short-term change in behavior that will produce measurable results while expressing concern and understanding for the difficulties the change presents to staff. A principal requesting a cross-disciplinary emphasis on nonfiction writing would sound something like this:

> *We've all heard the research on the power of writing to improve student achievement, but I want you to know that I heard the skepticism very clearly. You're busy, and besides, most of you are not trained as teachers of writing. So, I'm not asking you for buy-in right now. I'm just asking for a fair chance. You choose the day, you choose the prompt, and you choose how or whether to grade it. All I'm asking is that once each month for the next four months, you have a nonfiction writing prompt linked to your curriculum. Perhaps you will ask students to explain a graph in mathematics, describe a map in social studies, or detail an experiment in science. I'm asking you to use our very brief, simplified rubric—it's only about a third of a page. We should all expect students to write coherently, spell correctly, and support their claim with evidence in every subject. You are the subject experts and can assess content however you wish. I promise we'll then look at the results at the end of the semester and evaluate for ourselves whether the national research on nonfiction writing is relevant to our school.*
>
> *To be clear, I know that many of you are skeptical, and I value and respect skeptics. Skeptics brought us the Enlightenment. Skeptics*

brought us the Scientific Revolution. Skepticism is how we learn
and grow. So, it's OK to be skeptical—but let's give this a fair try and
learn together what works best for our students in our school.

I've seen similar progress through short-term changes in grading reform—a deeply emotional subject with strong opposition from many teachers. Rather than implementing an overhaul of grading systems that inevitably creates tension among faculty and parents, leaders hoping to effect change should start small. I've seen very skeptical teachers make presentations to their colleagues about small changes in their grading systems. For example, my interviews with educators who are skeptical about changing professional practices but are willing to consider incremental changes consist of conversations like this one:

I wasn't ready to change everything, but I just changed two things. I
stopped using the average to calculate semester grades, and I went
back to our old-fashioned A, B, C, D, F grading scale—just like we
calculate grade-point averages—with A = 4, B = 3, C = 2, D = 1, and
F = 0. I got rid of the one-hundred-point scale. That was it—just
those two changes, and this semester, with the same curriculum
and same assessments, I had more than forty fewer Ds and Fs. It
really made a difference. Students who used to fail were willing
to show resilience, work hard, and achieve at higher levels. I also
noticed that student behavior was significantly better because I
didn't have students who had just emotionally checked out due to
certain failure.

I could have given a thousand speeches on grading that wouldn't be as effective as this one teacher speaking to his colleagues about evidence from students in his school.

In the excellent book called *Atomic Habits*, author James Clear (2018) creates a powerful evidence-based approach about how individuals and organizations change. It is not through massive changes, but through incremental improvements with measurable results. No five-year goals. No bizarrely complicated strategic plans. No improvement plans that sit on the shelf. It's simply performing frequent actions—like writing just once a month or making small improvements in grading practices widely accepted as reasonable and showing results in a single semester. Let's drop the illusion of buy-in and just have respectful and evidence-based discussions with our colleagues.

Leaders and teachers can apply the idea that small changes lead to outsized results in order to make changes in high-poverty schools. To stay with the example of requesting nonfiction writing, a teacher may initially think, "I'll never have time to do this! It's just one more harebrained idea from administrators who don't know what it's like in my classroom. My students can barely read and speak English—how can we ask them to write?"

The key to responding to such concerns is *reframing*. The first step in reframing this response might be to just assess the accuracy of the teacher's statement, "I'll never have time." That is quite true if the request for writing is simply added to the day. But thoughtful equity and excellence school leaders are well aware of the need for focus (Reeves, 2011b; Schmoker, 2011). Therefore, before adding a writing strategy, leaders should very clearly outline the work and time commitment involved. Such a conversation may sound like this:

> *This writing assessment will take about twenty minutes per month to administer and about two hours to score collaboratively with colleagues. We already have a literacy block of one hundred minutes every day, for a total of about two thousand minutes each month. I'm asking that teachers use the first Wednesday of the month to administer an on-demand nonfiction writing prompt. Grade-level teachers can collaborate to choose the prompt and may want to have the prompt respond to content in science one month, social studies another month, and so on. That will be a decision left to each team. In order to provide the two hours to score, I'm changing the two monthly staff meetings to a five-minute brief on critical issues; the rest of those meetings will be allocated to collaborative scoring. We'll still have the meetings at the same times we have scheduled, but teachers will use that time for scoring.*

Reframing the original objection may not gain acceptance or offer insight. Rather, the response might sound something like:

> *I still am not convinced that nonfiction writing is a good idea, but at least I can see that we can do this once a month and that we'll have time to score it collaboratively—but I still want to see the evidence that this is any good!*

That's all that we need! Not perfect harmony, just a small change in professional practice so we can evaluate its impact on student performance.

What about the objection that students struggling with reading and speaking English shouldn't be asked to write? Reframing this response might sound something like this:

> *I guess the reality is that some students do better than others, and even the ones who are struggling with English can do something—at least a few sentences. In fact, some of the students struggling with English seem less stressed when I ask them to write rather than speak because they can write at their own pace, ask for help in finding the right words, and express themselves more comfortably than is sometimes the case with oral responses in class.*

People need trustworthy change models, and often teachers have a high level of distrust about external research and professional development because they are not always relevant to the students in their classrooms. Who are the most trustworthy messengers for effective practice? The teachers themselves. For example, when science teacher Steven Flitch originally contemplated changes to grading policies in his high-poverty school, he was resistant—the classic sit-in-the-back, arms folded, skeptical teacher. So doubtful was Mr. Flitch of proposed changes in grading policies that he kept two sets of books, so if the new ideas did not work out, he could easily return to his previous practices. But after a single semester, the results were overwhelming. Dramatically fewer student failures and Ds, and significantly more Cs and Bs. Of equal importance, Mr. Flitch reported when he focused grading on achievement of standards rather than accumulating points, the conversations with students changed dramatically, from "point-grubbing to learning" (S. Flitch, personal communication, January 4, 2019).

It is important to note that reframing is not a clever artifice to trick people into agreeing with a change initiative. Skeptics are skeptics for a reason—they have seen many "hot" initiatives come and go with little impact on student results. Reframing, however, exposes the concerns of the skeptics to factual analysis. *Knowledge illusion* is when people are irrationally and inaccurately convinced of things that are simply not true (Sloman & Fernbach, 2017). However deep the divisions within a faculty and however strenuous the objections to equity and excellence practices may be, the ultimate way to resolve these issues is with a commitment to truth. If you are confronted with a person who says, "I don't care what the evidence says; I'm just not going to believe it," the reframing approach will be ineffective because there is no agreement that truth is the basis for professional decision making. In these situations, you have an issue of professional conduct that is potentially dangerous and should be handled at the discretion of the schools and leaders. Presumably, such cases will be rare, and any use of reframing with true concern and understanding for the skeptics' fears, combined with evidence from their own classrooms, should be an effective method of managing change.

Summary

This chapter explored how equity and excellence schools engage in change in new and exciting ways, rejecting traditional change models that consume too much time and too many resources without results, and replacing them with a new change model that provides respect for the skeptics, deep and immediate implementation, and sustainable system change. Although the roles of leaders and policymakers are critical in making these changes, the actual implementation comes down to the classroom teacher. In every equity and excellence school, there are teacher leaders who use effective modeling, rather than administrative authority, to lead the way for gains in excellence and equity.

CHAPTER 12

Transform Vision Into Action Through Teacher Leadership

The previous chapter (page 99) discussed the concept of successfully effecting change, noting that if change is required, the answer is immediate action. The most likely change stems not from hierarchy or lectures, but rather from the direct observation of others who face the same challenges—evidence-based results. That is why leadership is not about command and control; it's about the improvement system architecture.

This chapter will discuss a third critical aspect of applying the equity and excellence teaching practices in schools—*teacher leadership*. Simply knowing the right practices to perform is not enough; to actualize results, effective leadership is needed at every level, including the teacher level. We begin by discussing new definitions of *leadership*, which allow teachers (who are actually in the classrooms with the students) to take the lead in making and assessing change. We will then learn about one proven method of teacher leadership—the science fair approach—and how it is an example of how *behavior precedes belief* and allows teachers to see the equity and excellence practices results with their own students in their own schools. Seeing these results will inevitably lead to buy-in. Finally, we will observe some case studies of teacher leadership in equity and excellence schools, learning lessons from the very individuals who have been improving student achievement in high-poverty schools.

Redefining Leadership

Founder of Lead From Within (https://lollydaskal.com) Lolly Daskal (2016) provides one hundred definitions of leadership from a variety of contemporary and ancient sources, including philosophers, military and political leaders, and a bevy of leadership theorists. A common theme is the need for vision, inspiration, and most of all, persuading others to do something that needs to be done. A few of the definitions include the following.

- "A leader is best when people barely know he exists, when his work is done, his aim fulfilled, they will say: we did it ourselves." —Lao Tzu

- "It is better to lead from behind and to put others in front, especially when you celebrate victory when nice things occur. You take the front line when there is danger. Then people will appreciate your leadership." —Nelson Mandela

- "Leadership and learning are indispensable to each other." —John F. Kennedy

- "The greatest leader is not necessarily the one who does the greatest things. He is the one that gets the people to do the greatest things." —Ronald Reagan

- "Leadership is the capacity to translate vision into reality." —Warren Bennis

- "Leadership defines what the future should look like, aligns people with that vision, and inspires them to make it happen, despite the obstacles." —John P. Kotter

- "Effective leadership is not about making speeches or being liked; leadership is defined by results, not attributes." —Peter F. Drucker

- "Innovation distinguishes between a leader and a follower." —Steve Jobs

- "Leadership is the art of mobilizing others to want to struggle for shared aspirations." —James M. Kouzes and Barry Z. Posner

- "A leader is one who knows the way, goes the way, and shows the way." —John Maxwell

- "Effective leadership is putting first things first. Effective management is discipline, carrying it out." —Stephen Covey

- "Leadership is a matter of how to be, not how to do it." —Frances Hesselbein

- "Leadership requires using power to influence the thoughts and actions of other people." —Abraham Zaleznik

- "That is what leadership is all about: staking your ground ahead of where opinion is and convincing people, not simply following the popular opinion of the moment." —Doris Kearns Goodwin

These definitions seem reasonable enough, and many are from people I admire deeply. Perhaps this definition synthesizes the best of the best definitions: *Leaders are the architects of improved individual and organizational performance.* This definition of *leader-as-architect* has some important implications.

First, the architect is the designer but does not lay bricks, operate cranes, or pound nails. Although some architects have these skills, they are usually wise enough to defer to their colleagues in the building trades whose skills vastly exceed their own. Second, the architect is, by definition, dissatisfied with things as they are. Whether the project is a new building or the renovation of an old one, the goal of the architect is one of improvement, not maintenance.

Third, this definition of leadership encompasses both the individual and the organization. Each person on the team must improve, and the organization as a whole must improve, or else the job is not finished. There is another analogy to building that is particularly apt in any consideration of effective leadership. Carpenters know that the way to strengthen a joist, beam, or other load-bearing part of a construction project is by *sistering* it—beefing up a weak or sagging piece of wood with additional support (Korpella, n.d.). A leader is not, as most definitions imply, a singular force of command and persuasion, but rather an architect who can *sister* the organization, providing support where necessary. The final implication of the leader-as-architect is the *vision is explicit.* Consider the architect's vision expressed in blueprints, drawings, and models. Contrast the clarity of these designs with the vision statements of many schools and educational systems. The people who design these vision statements may mean well, but many contain the same blurry mess of buzzwords, catch phrases, and personal priorities of the team members who wrote them. No bridge, office building, home, or backyard playhouse would last long if the architect's blueprints were as vague as most vision statements.

One of the best examples of transforming vision into action is by using the *science fair approach* to enable teacher leadership. In this approach, the vision is clear, empowering teachers to identify challenges, implement effective interventions, and be publicly accountable for results. Taking this vision and putting it into action is the subject of the next sections.

Encouraging the Science Fair Approach

We have all seen a science fair—students proudly display their research questions, express hypotheses, test those hypotheses, and show results. This format for school science fairs dates back to at least 1942 (Westinghouse Science Talent Search, n.d.), although the scientific method has been in use since Roger Bacon introduced it in the 13th century, and since the time of inductive and deductive reasoning by ancient civilizations in the Arabic- and Greek-speaking world. So, presenting a question, testing a hypothesis, and showing results is hardly a novel idea. Nevertheless, it remains relatively rare in education, at least outside university settings. But when *teachers* (not students) break through their reluctance to publicly engage in science fair projects, there are enormous advances in professional learning, improved professional practices, and, most important, better student results.

As previously stated, the format for the science fair is consistent. Each display has three panels.

1. **Left panel:** Challenge

2. **Middle panel:** Intervention (or Professional Practices)

3. **Right panel:** Results

Although leaders set the science fair framework, teachers express enormous degrees of creativity in determining the challenges and interventions, as well as how to assess the results. This process brings outstanding professional practices out of the shadows and into the light of day where others can examine and, where appropriate, replicate them. Sometimes this occurs at an individual school, with individual teachers or grade-level and department teams forming the science fair boards. Other times these events occur at the district, state, or provincial level. Whatever the scale, the format remains consistent: challenge, intervention, results.

The following examples of the science fair approach to change illustrate the power of teacher leadership. In each case, teachers used the same three-panel format of challenge, intervention, and result. These examples are a synthesis of hundreds I have observed.

- **Challenge:** Third-grade students were reading significantly below grade level.
- **Intervention:** We implemented deliberate reading strategies in every subject. This included marginal notes in books, summaries after paragraphs, and discussions with a book buddy. We replicated these strategies not only during reading time but also with our science and social studies texts.
- **Results:** At the beginning of the school year, only two out of thirty-four students were reading on grade level. By January, fourteen of thirty-four students were. By May, twenty-one students were on grade level.

- **Challenge:** Seventh-grade mathematics students were failing because they did not understand the challenges in the story problem format.
- **Intervention:** We implemented mathematics journals in which students recorded, in their home language, the specific mathematics challenge, such as a two-step equation. They created a story problem in their home language that used the specific mathematics challenge at hand. Then they created the same problem expressed in English.
- **Results:** At the beginning of the year, none of the English language learners (eighteen of the thirty-two students in the class) were on grade level for mathematics. By January, six were. By the end of the year, thirteen of the eighteen English language learners were on grade level.

- **Challenge:** There was chronic absenteeism in K–12 classes, with more than 30 percent of students missing eighteen or more days the previous year.
- **Intervention:** We implemented *60-second reports*, in which every missing student's family was called within 60 seconds of the beginning of the school day. We stopped using robocalls or afternoon calls from attendance clerks and started using *all hands*—that is, everyone not engaged in instruction—calls one minute after the beginning of the school day. In addition, we provided supplementary transportation and offered additional support to students and parents to pursue the goal of 100 percent on-time attendance.
- **Results:** Within the first two months of school, the chronic absentee rate dropped from more than 30 percent to less than 10 percent.

Using the science fair method addresses some of the most persistent objections to applying educational research in a local school or classroom. It nullifies claims like

"The national research doesn't apply to us" and "Our students are different" because the students are in the teachers' own classrooms and schools. They are from the same families and neighborhoods. The schools have the same per-pupil funding, labor agreement, teacher assignment policy, curriculum, and assessments. The only difference in student results is related to specific changes in teacher professional practices—the interventions teachers provide to students. The science fair method also addresses any concerns about commercial interests corrupting the research because the researchers are the teachers who have no agenda except to improve student achievement.

Some teachers may object to conducting research in their own classrooms because they believe research is trying to make education a science, when it is really an art. Although Robert J. Marzano (2017) makes it clear these two descriptors of teaching—*art* and *science*—are not mutually exclusive, there is a danger when the discipline relies too heavily on the art of teaching. While some parts of teaching are difficult to measure, particularly regarding the genuine love of students, there are many objectively observable elements of teaching. We can observe the frequency with which students receive feedback, the accuracy of that feedback, and the student responses to the feedback. We can observe the frequency and impact of nonfiction writing. We can observe the resilience of students when they work harder and resubmit work as a result of a teacher-revised grading policy. One reason it is so important to define with clarity that interventions are part of effective teaching is that it shifts the focus from the practitioner to the practice, or from the teacher to the teaching (Marshall, 2005). When the focus is on the teacher, the presumption is that an "effective teacher" has a positive impact on student results. As alluring as this presumption sounds, it has been tested and found wanting (Strauss, 2013).

The problem with rating teachers is that today's grade A teachers can be tomorrow's grade D teachers, and vice versa. Changes in labels of teacher effectiveness have more to do with changes in student populations and other variables than with the teacher. However, when the focus is on *teaching*—the objectively observable practices of the teacher—there is far more consistency linking causes to effects, and practices to student performance. Year in and year out, quality feedback is linked to improved student performance; improved grading practices are linked to better motivation, performance, attendance, and discipline; and higher-quality writing is associated with improved understanding. The science fair approach does not say, "Look at this amazing teacher! She is so extraordinary!" Rather, the science fair approach says, "Look at this amazing teaching practice! It's something that you can also do with the students in your school and classroom."

Finally, a note about what *results* mean in the context of the science fair approach. Originally, *results* meant simple bar graphs showing before-and-after scores. Some charts compared the previous semester to the current one, or compared the same students to their own previous results. Other charts compared similar groups of students, but from different years. Although my own research experience tends toward the quantitative, I have learned not everything that counts can (or should) be counted. Some of the most impressive before-and-after displays of results I have seen were not a comparison of assessment results, but rather actual student work showing how, over time with effective teaching interventions, the same student progressed. These displays of results showed, for example, comparisons of the student's fall, winter, and spring writing skills. An observer could watch as the same student, with the same background, challenges, and home circumstances—indeed, every single variable the same—improves dramatically over the course of the school year. The same observations could apply to a student's mathematical problem solving, inferences from science lab experiments, and critical analyses of historical documents. These qualitative displays show in compelling fashion the impact of effective teaching practices and explicit interventions on the performance of students.

Teachers in high poverty schools are weary of programs and systems that do not take into account the needs of their students and environments. The use of teacher leadership, illustrated by the science fair approach, allows teachers to implement change effectively because they have vivid evidence of the fact that the proposed changes have been effective in their schools, with their students, and in their communities.

Understanding Teacher Leadership in the Equity and Excellence Context

Schools in some of the most challenging settings in North America (some with 90 to 100 percent of students qualifying for free or reduced-price lunch, some with more than 90 percent of students identified as English language learners, and all with more than 90 percent of students members of ethnic minority groups) embrace the science fair approach to improve professional practices and student results. These include schools in urban, suburban, and rural environments. Some schools are very small—only about two hundred students—while others are large, comprehensive high schools with thousands of students. All of them have strong unions, and the administrators and bargaining units take teachers' rights and responsibilities seriously. None of these schools have exceptional funding; indeed, budget cuts, large class sizes, and inadequate resources are the norm, not the exception. And yet they consistently demonstrate outstanding gains in student achievement explicitly linked to effective teaching practices.

If you could pick the trifecta of resistance to change, it would include this formula: take three twenty-year veteran teachers; put them in a high school environment where their independence has been a matter of tradition, policy, and state law; add in the most volatile and emotionally laden subject in American education—grading reform—and easily predict that any change effort is a nonstarter. Yet this describes the situation in the United States' second-poorest school system, San Bernardino City Unified School District in California. Once a prospering town with industry, a U.S. Air Force base, and substantial government employment, the years from 1990 to 2010 witnessed the steady decline of the city into poverty. High school failure rates were particularly high, with an estimated 40 percent of students arriving in ninth grade reading below grade level. Not surprisingly, this resulted in high failure rates, especially for students struggling not only with academic skills but also with English literacy fundamentals. Moreover, in high school, the most significant causes of failing grades were students not completing homework or, having failed a test, having no hope of ultimately becoming proficient on California standards. These challenges were particularly acute in mathematics and science, where failure rates of 30 to 60 percent were common.

In 2018, when the district first considered ways to address these challenges, there was understandable skepticism. Like most high-poverty systems, teachers and administrators had heard many outside experts attempt to tell them how to fix their problems, and the cynicism and distrust of one more round of educational reforms was palpable. But this time, the district did not look to outsiders; rather, the district's own teachers (as leaders) used the science fair approach to develop pilot projects. With support of the union, teachers volunteered to design and lead pilot projects, and the results were stunning. Michael Doll, who teaches ninth- and tenth-grade mathematics, was blunt about the challenge he faced: more than forty students failing every semester. The interventions he considered were straightforward: eliminate the use of the average to calculate the final score, target reassessment for students not yet proficient on standards, relentlessly focus on hard work to gain proficiency, and eliminate homework and class participation as parts of the grade. To ensure against grade inflation, Mr. Doll continued to use the same final exam as in the past, along with the same rigorous mathematics curriculum and assessment system. The results speak from themselves: in the first semester he implemented his reforms, failures went from more than forty to zero.

Veteran science teacher Steven Flitch was also a skeptic, describing himself to me as "the guy in the back of the room with his arms folded" when the district initially contemplated the science fair idea. But, as a scientist, he agreed to conduct the experiment and consider the results. While some students still failed, the number of failures dropped dramatically. Interestingly, because his standards were now crystal clear and very rigorous, not only did fewer students fail but fewer also earned A grades. Why? Because achievement in the class was no longer an exercise in accumulating points and playing the game of school well; the focus was on learning. Finally, Tom Pham, another science teacher, experienced similar results, but also noticed an impact on discipline, with student tardiness virtually eliminated and classroom culture dramatically improved.

The results these three educators developed were mirrored in some of the highest-poverty districts in Connecticut—New Haven, East Hartford, Bristol, Hartford, and Bridgeport. With a laser-like focus, they created science fair displays in January 2019 showing consistent and significant gains in literacy. It is particularly significant that these teachers included science fair findings for kindergarten, first, and second grades, because the K–2 grades continuum is invisible in most U.S. state-level accountability systems; states only begin reporting student data in third grade. And yet, these educators knew that success in later grades begins in preK and kindergarten, and they courageously displayed results even though they had no impact on external accountability results. In brief, they were accountable not because any external authority required them to be accountable, but simply because it was the right thing to do.

The science fair approach has been widely replicated in rural, suburban, and urban high-poverty systems in Missouri, Wisconsin, Nevada, and Virginia. One of the widely misunderstood demographic stereotypes is that schools labeled *suburban* are wealthy. But the data tell a different story. Educational systems in what were the bucolic suburbs of decades past now are home to some of the same challenges of poverty, unemployment, fragmented families, substance abuse, and more that plague their urban counterparts. The good news is, like their colleagues who have long been serving urban schools, teachers in suburban and rural systems adapt the equity and excellence techniques to meet their needs. They systematically identify, document, and replicate practices in ways clearly identified as effective on their home turf. In *Reframing Teacher Leadership to Improve Your School*, I provide additional case studies about elementary, middle, and high school classrooms that adopted the science fair approach (Reeves, 2008b). The essence of these findings is *the right practice is not enough.* It takes effective leadership at every level, including teacher leadership, to transform research into practice.

Summary

Too often the phrase *teacher leadership* is code for "giving teachers administrative responsibilities without paying them more." Real teacher leadership, as this chapter shows, is about elevating the most effective teaching practices to the audience that matters most—their fellow teachers. We considered the science fair method for how teachers systematically share their challenges, interventions, and results. Most important, we considered how this practice, begun with the original equity and excellence schools, has now been widely replicated across the United States. We now turn our attention to how teachers and leaders can find professional sustenance not from administrative imperatives, but from effective coaching, feedback, and evaluation.

CHAPTER 13

Improve Coaching, Feedback, and Evaluation

The evidence presented thus far makes clear that feedback for students must meet four criteria: fair, accurate, specific, and timely. I have asked teachers and administrators around the world about their best and worst experiences in receiving feedback. They consistently return to these criteria. Their worst experiences were when feedback was inconsistent—that is, the same performance received either positive or negative feedback from a supervisor. It was clearly unfair. They complained that feedback did not accurately represent their work—that is, it was inaccurate. Even positive feedback, such as a sticky note with "Good job!" written on it, was insufficiently specific. Worst of all, feedback was often late and ineffectual. In many schools, the last few weeks of the school year are consumed by a frantic document drill in which administrators provide feedback on classroom observations and other teacher activities that occurred months earlier. These criteria for student feedback—fair, accurate, specific, and timely—are effective guidelines for coaching and providing feedback to teachers and administrators.

This chapter is thus devoted to best practices for improving coaching, feedback, and evaluation practices. It begins by expounding the definition of *coaching,* including what coaching is *not,* and will discuss how to build capacity in those teachers being coached by using questions rather than answers. It will then discuss how leaders and teachers alike can utilize the powerful tool of feedback to maximize student achievement. Finally, we'll consider all three practices together—coaching, feedback, and evaluation—and discover how educators can use the three in conjunction for the greatest results.

Improving Coaching by Building Capacity With Questions, Not Answers

The term *coaching* is defined in many different ways and with equally ambiguous results as the term *leadership*. In many educational systems, the hallmarks of instructional coaching and leadership coaching are eerily similar to a therapeutic relationship. The engagement is voluntary; the client, not the coach, largely establishes the methodology; the conversations are confidential; and the focus is almost entirely on the individual receiving the coaching, not the needs of the organization providing the coaching. The agenda for coaching conversations often focuses on the personal needs, including emotional and psychological needs, of the client. These include well-intentioned but misguided attempts to address significant issues such as stress, anxiety, and depression. At other times, the coach is less like a therapist and more like a consultant. The client comes with questions and problems to solve, and the coach provides answers. Perhaps the most common form of coaching is when a supervisor wishes to provide "coaching," which almost invariably means evaluative feedback on performance. In fact, the coach is not a therapist, consultant, or supervisor. Rather, the coach is committed to a singular mission—the improvement of individual and organizational performance. This is directly parallel to the responsibilities of the leader.

The hallmarks of effective coaching include the following four characteristics. First, coaching is *individualized.* It is conducted in one-to-one sessions. While some group coaching sessions are possible with very experienced teams, the hierarchical nature of educational systems means each person in a group has a role and a rank. No matter how much a facilitator or coach may protest, those roles and ranks are persistent and pervade every discussion. In order to have a foundation of trust and integrity—the essence of any relationship—the coach must not inhibit the person being coached from acknowledging failure, seeking alternative solutions, and considering alternative points of view. In a group setting, these can be signs of weakness, while in individualized coaching sessions, they are signs of serious reflection and professional strength.

Second, coaching must be *sustained* over an extended period of time. The minimum coaching engagement leaders should consider is one year, with either one-hour monthly meetings or thirty-minute twice-monthly meetings. This time commitment is essential to build trust, consider alternatives, gather evidence, evaluate results, and make the midcourse corrections essential to improve performance. When I hear principals claim they have been coached once or twice a year, I don't know what those conversations are, but they are certainly not coaching.

Third, coaching is *content specific*. Beware the generalist who claims he or she can coach anyone about anything. There is a reason professionals specialize. There is simply too much to know in medicine, engineering, and law, for example, to credibly claim universal knowledge. Coaching high school mathematics teachers is different from coaching superintendents, which is different from coaching the leader of a kindergarten grade-level team. Although the coach is not a consultant providing advice, he or she must have a clear understanding of the environment, stressors, and challenges the client faces.

Fourth, coaching is *focused on deliberate and purposeful practice* that leads to the accomplishment of specific goals. The test of a coach is not whether the client likes the coach or enjoys a fun personal relationship with the coach. The test is the degree to which the individual being coached and the organization supporting the coaching process actually improve performance.

Effective coaches hold a mirror up to the client and, in every meeting, compare the goals of the client to the reality achieved. The reality may be that the goals are unclear ("I want to improve communication") or not compatible with the reality the client is facing ("I want the state to increase our budget"). The goals may be for factors outside the control of the client ("I want my colleagues to have better attitudes, and I want my students and parents to do more work at home"). Effective coaches, therefore, start with clear goals within the grasp of the client and, crucially, relevant to the most important individual and organization results.

Given how busy teachers in high-poverty schools are, it is little wonder that many say, "I just don't have time for coaching. I need to be in the classroom, write grants, comply with endless directives, and deal with students and parents. There just is not an extra hour in the month to do this." They are right, at least with regard to most coaching. But when done properly, coaching can have significant and positive effects. Author and researcher Joellen Killion (2017) reports:

> A meta-analysis of 37 studies of teacher coaching, many focused on literacy coaching, reveals that coaching positively affects both teaching practices and student achievement. The pooled effects of both general coaching and content-specific coaching have a positive and significant effect on teacher instruction as measured by classroom observations. Both general and content-specific coaching have a positive and significant effect on student achievement. (p. 20)

The evidence on coaching strongly supports a heavy dose of assessment and then application of those assessment results to the client's objectives. Evidence strongly supports two assessments: Gallup's *strengths-based coaching* (as cited in Rath, 2007) and *renewal coaching* (Allison & Reeves, 2012; Reeves & Allison, 2009, 2010). What both of these coaching assessments have in common is that the results strongly relate to both the client's job performance and personal and life satisfaction. In the case for *strengths-based coaching,* the evidence suggests people who are regularly coached on developing their strengths are several times more likely to report higher levels of job performance and personal satisfaction (as cited in Rath, 2007). In the case of *renewal coaching*, a study of more than one thousand educational leaders shows performance on the renewal and resilience scales are very strongly related to job performance and life satisfaction (Allison & Reeves, 2012; Reeves & Allison, 2009, 2010). The Gallup assessment is entirely quantitative and administered online (as cited in Rath, 2007; see www.gallup.com/cliftonstrengths/en/254033/strengthsfinder.aspx). Similar strengths-based assessments are available for free at the University of Pennsylvania website (see www.authentichappiness.sas.upenn.edu/testcenter). Renewal coaching assessments combine Likert-scale responses with open-ended responses; the latter may be very helpful in provoking deep coaching conversations.

Coaching is, unfortunately, the Wild West of professional services (Sherman & Freas, 2004) with no standards or consistent practice principles. Even certifications of coaches, which universities sometimes offer at a cost of tens of thousands of dollars, are no assurance the coach is engaged in the most effective forms of coaching. Therefore, it is the responsibility of the client to ask about process and practice and, most important, about the relationship between the coaching process and individual and organization results.

Building Capacity Through Feedback

Everyone needs feedback. It is the only way we navigate through life, reinforcing our best decisions and making midcourse corrections when we miss the mark. Imagine driving a car or, for that matter, walking down the street without feedback. In a car, a warning light might go on, presenting the driver with choices: either pull over, assess the impact of the warning, and take steps to remedy the warning, or take out a very tiny hammer and ensure the warning light never illuminates again. Similarly, when a walker or runner feels pain, he or she can ignore it, confident that he or she can work through the pain, or he or she can stop and assess it, distinguishing short-term discomfort from serious warning signs that call for a change in gait, stride, speed, distance, or elevation.

Feedback for teachers and leaders is as vital as feedback for drivers, runners, and walkers. Consider your own best and worst experiences with receiving feedback. When I ask teachers and leaders about this, the most common examples of terrible feedback I hear are the following.

- "The worst feedback? None at all. I never knew where I stood."

- "All I received was a 'Good job!' and a smiley face. I had no idea what that meant."

- "My boss saved up a year of criticism and delivered it at the end of the year, long after it was too late for me to do anything about it."

- "I received feedback different from my colleague, but we were both doing exactly the same thing."

One of the distinguishing characteristics of feedback in equity and excellence schools is that it is *FAST*—that is, fair, accurate, specific, and timely. These criteria for effective feedback apply to both students and adults. Let us consider each of these criteria and why they are so important.

Fairness is about consistency. Any reader who has been on a playground has heard the plaintive cry, "That's not fair!" A brief inquiry will usually reveal one child's interpretation and understanding of the rules of a game are different from the other children's. We see this in games adults play as well, with the crowd roaring its discontent every time an official applies a rule inconsistently. Most diehard sports fans can deal with a loss—that's part of the game. But they have a very hard time dealing with inconsistency, the essence of unfairness. And yet, this is precisely what happens to teachers when officials use mysterious criteria to evaluate them and those same officials walking through their classrooms are unable to articulate these criteria.

Some observation rubrics (such as those available from Kim Marshall at https://marshallmemo.com) are exceptionally specific, constructive, and consistent. But in many other cases, I have seen administrators demand *excellence in instruction* without articulating what it means. As these administrators wander through classrooms, sometimes with an entourage in tow, it is reminiscent of the Indian fable about the blind men and the elephant: several people blindly touch the same animal, but each comes away with entirely different ideas of what the animal is (Baldwin, 2011). This is no exaggeration, as fully-sighted observers can watch a classroom and come to three wildly different conclusions about the effectiveness of the instruction. Leadership assessment is even worse. In a large-scale study of leadership evaluations, I find leadership feedback is most effective for new administrative interns because it's immediate, specific, and constructive (Reeves, 2009a). But the longer their tenure and the higher their rank, the more ambiguous and less helpful the feedback. Indeed, some veteran principals and central office leaders have never been evaluated. Whether they are playing a game or dealing with threats to their careers, students, and teachers, leaders know most feedback is simply unfair. In equity and excellence schools, fairness in feedback is enhanced because of the commitment to collaborative scoring. Different teachers look at the same performance and provide the same—or at least very similar—feedback.

The second criterion of effective feedback is *accuracy*. The essence of accuracy is that evaluators are providing feedback on what they claim to be observing. In the case of students, teachers know the differences between observing student performance in mathematics and observing student performance in English language literacy that happens to have numbers in it. Teachers also know the differences between assessing reading comprehension and assessing content knowledge. A student's zip code, level of parental engagement, nutrition, quality of sleep, and a variety of other variables influence reading comprehension. In the case of teacher evaluation, feedback on performance focuses on what the teacher does, not variables beyond the teacher's control. In the case of administrators and central office leadership, feedback focuses on observable actions of those leaders, not external conditions to which they can respond, but can neither influence nor control.

The third criterion is *specificity*. Effective feedback allows the recipient to know precisely what to do to improve performance. This is the reason that scoring rubrics and checklists are so powerful. Without these tools, students are left to assume they are the factory workers and the teacher is the foreman, uniquely qualified to assess the quality of the submitted work. But with clearly specific scoring rubrics and checklists, written in accessible language, every student in the class is empowered to assess and, most important, respond to assessments with improved performance.

The fourth criterion for effective feedback is *timely*. Hattie (2009) suggests teachers conduct this simple test: ask students to predict their own grades. If they received a steady stream of feedback throughout a term, their predictions should be quite accurate. But in a surprising number of cases I have seen, students are astonished when they receive failing grades. This is true even when there are computerized grading systems that purport to give students all the information they need to know their performance levels. The model of timely feedback is the music director or athletic coach. They do not tell students about wrong notes or busted plays at the end of a term, but rather provide feedback within seconds of the performance. Many official evaluation practices for classroom teachers institutionalize poor and untimely feedback, allowing administrators to see only one or two classes during an entire year, and allowing weeks or even months to pass before the teacher sees the evaluation. These systems apparently presume administrators have forty-eight-hour days and teachers have mystical interpretation powers. And it's worse for administrators and central office leaders when it comes to timely feedback; it is not unusual for school leaders to be held accountable for the previous year's test scores, delivered long after it is possible for the them to make any changes in instruction, schedule, or intervention plans. Superintendents, if they receive evaluations at all, often receive feedback at the end of their contract.

Despite these challenges, feedback can be effective. In equity and excellence schools, the rule is *frequent feedback with collaborative scoring.* Student self-assessment is the rule, not the exception, and teachers have clear models of expected work quality and academic rigor. Leaders observe teachers very frequently—sometimes weekly—so there is no doubt about what effective professional practices are. Moreover, the use of collaborative teams in PLCs allows these schools to identify, document, and replicate their most effective practices. Leaders receive feedback not just from their central office supervisors, but from teachers, students, parents, and themselves. They need not wait until the end of the school year to know their feedback on professional practices and student results.

Adding the Final Step: Evaluation

To get the most out of coaching, feedback, and evaluation, we must be clear about the *purpose* and *practice.* Coaching is not therapy or vague interactions to meet private and personal aims, but a systematic means to assess individual needs, compare performance against goals, and thus improve individual and organization performance. Effective feedback is FAST—and these principles apply to students, teachers, and leaders.

Evaluation serves a very different purpose from coaching and feedback. Although evaluation systems are cumbersome, expensive, and time-consuming, there is no evidence they improve teaching and leadership. The reason is because the vast majority of teachers and leaders—well over 95 percent—are classified as effective or highly effective, even though the evidence suggests that in most organizations (including schools and districts), the actual percentage is lower. In New Jersey, more than 98 percent of teachers are rated effective or highly effective (State of New Jersey Department of Education, 2016), and in New York, the number exceeds 97 percent (Disare, 2017). Although I deeply admire my friends in the Garden and Empire states,

I know of few educators or administrators in those states who would argue that these numbers correspond to their observations. The reason is clear: if a teacher is not rated as effective or highly effective, they face dismissal, and the administrator providing low ratings will deal with the toxic cultural consequences that follow.

Moreover, there is no evidence I have seen that suggests evaluating people in any organization—education, business, nonprofit, religious, or otherwise—can lead them to better performance. A student who receives an F or zero does not smack a hand to his or her forehead and say, "Now I get it! I have seen the light! I will go forth and improve my performance!" Teachers who receive unsatisfactory evaluations are less likely to seek coaching for improvement than to seek legal counsel. Evaluations do not improve performance. Rather, coaching and feedback lead to better performance; that's where leaders and teachers should invest the vast majority of their time.

Summary

In this chapter, we considered some of the most powerful techniques to improve individual, school, and district performance. Coaching can have dramatic and positive effects, but only if it is defined clearly and implemented in a way that is clearly distinguished from feel-good faux therapy or quick-fix consulting. Feedback can be one of the most powerful tools teachers and leaders use, provided it is FAST (fair, accurate, specific, and timely). Evaluations have limited utility beyond compliance with state requirements and are never useful as a singular tool for improvement. Coaching and feedback, from the classroom to the superintendent's office, is a micro-level process that involves analyzing and responding to data for individual students, classrooms, and schools. This work is the foundation for the most challenging application of equity and excellence research and is a system-level change, the subject of part III. In the next section, we consider how effective accountability systems are vital to the implementation and sustainability of the equity and excellence solution.

PART IV

Creating Accountability in an Equity and Excellence System

Educational accountability is at a crossroads. To some people, the term *accountability* means that schools, along with the teachers and administrators within the schools, will be held accountable through a system of rewards and punishments associated with external indicators, such as test scores, graduate rates, discipline rates, student and parent surveys, attendance, and other factors. This cycle of punishment and reward based on external metrics depends entirely on the relationship of the factors that are measured to the goals of the system. Bina Venkataraman (2019) explains this challenge through the story of an

MIT colleague who was given a device to track her steps, under the theory that more steps were associated with better health. Departments competed against one another to achieve the greatest number of steps. Venkataraman's colleague dutifully increased her step count every afternoon, including a trek past a bakery, where she would stop to purchase a couple of pastries. Her department won the competition, even as her colleague's weight and sugar intake increased. In the educational context, there are more sinister examples of the consequences of measuring the wrong things, with cheating, narrowing of the curriculum, and mindless test preparation taking the place of a rich and rigorous curriculum, all in the pursuit of the test measures on which the local accountability system focuses. I have witnessed schools move their most effective teachers to the tested grades and away from non-tested grades, such as kindergarten, even though it is axiomatic that kindergarten is a key foundation for future success.

It doesn't have to be this way. This section is not a screed against educational accountability, but rather a plea to get accountability *right*. Rather than a system that is designed to punish and reward educators, accountability can be a learning system, identifying the professional practices and other factors that contribute to and detract from student performance.

My original research (Reeves, 2004) identified the original equity and excellence schools and practices because the district had established a new comprehensive accountability system. Unlike most accountability systems that focus only on test scores, this system focused on *causes*—the specific actions of teachers and leaders—not just effects. If educators only had test scores, they would never learn about the value of nonfiction writing, collaborative scoring, and the other equity and excellence schools hallmarks.

In the United States, the Every Student Succeeds Act (ESSA) specifically allows states to expand the meaning of *accountability* to include factors far beyond test scores, including student participation in the arts, extracurricular activities, and service. Moreover, ESSA specifically invites states to consider growth in student achievement and not merely the percentage of students who achieve proficient scores on state tests (DuFour, Reeves, & DuFour, 2018). This can include not only performance in the arts, service, and extracurricular activities but also the causes of achievement and engagement, including what teachers and leaders do. We can go beyond the tautology that plagues teacher observations (that is, *Good teachers have higher student test scores*) and instruct teachers that, in order to be good, they must *attain* higher student test scores. This circular reasoning has shed no light at all on what specifically teachers and leaders need *to do* to improve student achievement. Moreover, the myopic focus on annual literacy and mathematics test scores in grades 3–8 provides no insight into how teachers can make instantaneous improvement in their instruction, curriculum, and assessment practices. Fortunately, ESSA explicitly allows for this sort of alternative accountably system, if only U.S. state boards of education will take advantage of the flexibility they have before them (DuFour et al., 2018).

The chapters in this section will discuss how to get educational accountability right in your school. Chapter 14 will focus on how to establish accountability as a learning system, rather than a humiliation mechanism. Chapters 15 and 16 will then discuss how to implement accountability at first the system level, then the school and department levels. Finally, chapter 17 will discuss the equally important aspect of explaining the story behind the data to the relevant stakeholders.

Establish Accountability as a Learning System

What do the statements "We're going to hold schools accountable" or "We must hold teachers accountable" imply to you? When these kinds of statements emanate from a U.S. state legislator who advocates for school choice, for example, the implication is that the schools' ratings—often expressed in letter grades from A to F—be public so parents can make informed choices for their children. Who, after all, would willingly send their child to a substandard school with a low grade? When you hear a similar statement from a school board member directed at the superintendent, it usually implies the leader's job depends on producing results however the school board defines them. When teachers use the statement, "I'm going to hold you accountable" to students, it often implies a consequence, such as a low grade for missing work or poor performance on a test. In sum, *accountability*, as it is most commonly known in the public discourse about education, is almost always associated with exposure, threats, intimidation, and punishments.

Just as teachers cannot threaten or humiliate students into good performance, when leaders apply these tactics toward adults, the result is more likely resentment rather than inspiration to better performance. In the most tragic circumstances, accountability as an instrument to threaten, humiliate, and terminate employees can lead to cheating and a series of ruined careers and lives. The Atlanta Public Schools cheating scandal not only affected those caught cheating but also threw a shadow over the legitimate achievements of many hardworking students, teachers, and administrators (Blinder, 2015). This can happen when accountability is no more than test scores, but it doesn't have to be that way. Educational leaders can change the purpose of accountability from a system to rate, rank, sort, label, and fire teachers and administrators to a fundamentally new system—one to assist in the improvement of teaching, learning, and leadership. When the purpose of accountability is changed in this way, a learning system emerges in which every stakeholder can embrace, rather than fear, accountability.

This chapter will provide readers with an understanding of how accountability functions in equity and excellence schools and the positive effect accountability can have on student achievement. It will discuss how accountability provides the missing link in many change initiatives by allowing educators to understand the *causes* behind the numbers. Finally, it will present the components of an accountability learning system, including the district-, school-, and department-level indicators leaders can use to track, measure, and demonstrate the success or failure of a teaching practice.

Understanding Accountability in Equity and Excellence Schools

The original equity and excellence studies (Reeves, 2004) began with what my colleagues and I thought was an error. Along with data analysts, I looked at data from more than one hundred schools in one of the United States' largest urban systems (Milwaukee Public Schools). Predictably, the higher the percentage of students eligible for free or reduced-price lunch, the lower the achievement levels. You can envision the graph showing poverty on the horizontal axis and achievement on the vertical axis, with a little dot for every school. The dots form a neat line from the upper left to the lower right. In the analysis, it's clear that higher poverty means lower achievement— except for a cluster of dots in the upper right corner of the graph. Because the dots are on the right side, the schools are also high-poverty schools, but because they are at the top of the graph, the data suggest these schools are also high performing, with more than 90 percent of students meeting standards on recent assessments. Perhaps it's a mistake, we thought, so I undertook further analysis of the data and then went on site visits to each of these high-poverty, high-achieving schools.

The context of this discovery was during the district's development of its own pioneering accountability system. Like most districts, the term *accountability* was little more than an assemblage of test scores, along with data on attendance and behavior plus student demographic characteristics. It was the district's creation of a new accountability system—one that includes specific and observable actions of teachers and leaders, not just test scores—that allowed a systematic examination of the factors that led to equity and excellence performance. This is especially important because, without this systematic assessment for causes, the only causes found in the accountability system were student demographic data. Effective teaching and leadership were invisible.

As other U.S. schools replicated the equity and excellence findings, two important ideas emerged. First, the relationship between student poverty and student performance declined dramatically. Rather than the usual line (from the upper left to the lower right, showing that more poverty inevitably means lower achievement), the line began to flatten out. In Norfolk, Virginia, and Wayne Township, Indiana, the relationship between poverty and student achievement was nearly zero. The most important variables in determining student results were not student demographics, but effective teaching and leadership. It is no surprise that Norfolk won the Broad Prize for the best urban system in the United States, and Wayne Township won the Magna Award from the National School Boards Association for the superior board policymaking that led to effective accountability and improved results.

Second, in 2018, Newark Public Schools in New Jersey began a campaign under the leadership of Superintendent Roger León to publicly disclose data on every school, something not done since the 1990s prior to his taking of the district helm in July 2018. One of the most stunning findings as Newark began its development of a new accountability system was that, contrary to popular assumptions, student demographics did not predict student achievement. Indeed, the most powerful variable in predicating low achievement was teacher turnover. Teachers do not quit *jobs*; they quit *managers* (Brenneman, 2016). Therefore, a central challenge for Newark was to improve leadership effectiveness at every level and improve the schools' culture so teachers would want to remain, thus providing a consistent and emotionally safe environment for students.

Having an effective accountability system does not guarantee a district will generate equity and excellence schools. But accountability is the key to finding, documenting, and replicating the most effective practices that lead to equity and excellence performance.

Revealing the Causes of Student Achievement

The Centers for Disease Control and Prevention (CDC) has a Healthy Schools initiative, one part of which is a school-based measurement of each student's body mass index (BMI). Imagine this well-intentioned health effort became part of a school's accountability report card. Well, you don't need to imagine it, as more than 25 percent of U.S. schools are gathering these data (Lohmann, 2015). There are good reasons for wanting to learn this, as childhood obesity rates are at an all-time high (Lohmann, 2015). Parents and voters are rightfully concerned about their children's health just as much as they are about their reading scores. But with BMI numbers, we have only effects, not causes. If the BMI goes down, as most parents hope, they might also want to know about causes. Did BMI decline because the school had a splendid exercise program and promoted healthy eating choices, or did the BMI decline because the students were no longer interested in food as a result of eating disorders or drug addictions? Placed in this context, most parents would be interested in those causes, not just the BMI scores. Similarly, parents are rightfully concerned about low reading scores in many schools, but we should learn more about the causes of low scores. A low score might occur because the teachers and principals are failing to apply a scientifically based reading curriculum. Scores might be low because the schedule doesn't allow teachers time to implement even the most effective curriculum. The scores might be low because there are more students in the classroom than there are available desks and books. Scores might be low because the district's special education program has such an excellent reputation that a disproportionately high number of parents of children with learning disabilities send them to schools in that district. For every effect—in this case, low reading scores—there are many possible causes. An accountability system that fails to include an analysis of causes is as bad as a health system that can't tell the difference between a good diet and an eating disorder.

Chapter 16 (page 155) will address in greater detail how schools and educational systems can link causes and effects, and the science fair examples from equity and excellence schools are illustrative. What accounts for the improved ninth- and tenth-grade mathematics scores in San Bernardino, California? Perhaps it was *grade inflation*—teachers just handing out higher grades to avoid any controversy with the administration. Perhaps they lowered standards, so it was easier for more students to show proficiency without doing more work. An effects-based accountability system would not consider these alternative causes. But in the causes-based system that San Bernardino is developing, it's very clear how effects link to causes. Teachers demonstrate, through the use of consistent assessments and final exams, there is no grade inflation. Because they maintain the same standards and curricula, there is no lowering of standards. And most important, because teachers document their professional practices, they can show the specific classroom practices and grading policies that lead to higher student achievement. This is not advanced statistical analysis; it is simply showing student performance data before and after teachers implement specific professional practices.

Why do some schools have significantly better reading scores, even though the students have the same demographic characteristics as lower-achieving counterparts? The answer could be extra money, a different teacher assignment policy, or a principal with different personality traits. But an accountability system that tests these assumptions allows for a deeper dive into causes. The per-pupil funding was the same; the teacher assignment policy was the same; and the principals in equity and excellence schools are ebullient and quiet, introverts and extroverts, scholastically inclined and sports fanatics. None of those purported causes explain reaching higher achievement. The distinguishing features are none of these things, but rather high levels of nonfiction writing, more effective teacher collaboration, and the laser-like focus on achievement, to name a few equity and excellence practices. An examination of causes not only identifies what professional practices are most important but also excludes hypothetical causes people often consider, but rarely test.

Identifying the Components of a Learning System

A learning system requires three levels of analysis. First, the district or other system-level leadership must identify *the results to achieve*. These results typically include board priorities, such as academic achievement, safety, attendance, and other key indicators that form the basis for safe and effective schools. Some boards intently focus on just a few variables; other boards have more than one hundred such system-level variables, with the latter typically stemming from strategic planning exercises that overwhelm the board and senior leadership with goals, objectives, action plans, and performance indicators.

The second component of a learning system is to identify *school and department indicators*. These are the *cause* indicators—that is, the specific actions of teachers and administrators related to the *effect* indicators at the system level. While the system-level indicators apply to every school, the cause indicators will vary from one school to another. Some schools need to address effective implementation of their literacy program, while others may need to focus on parent involvement, and still others may need to focus on effective instruction delivery. My review of school improvement plans reveals some school plans had more than seventy separate priorities, and it was not unusual to find twenty or more (Reeves, 2011b). However, schools with six or fewer priorities show significantly better gains in academic achievement over three years. Therefore, I recommend schools in a learning system have no more than six indicators. At the end of each year, the administration examines the relationship between causes and effects and then shares that information districtwide. That is what makes accountability a learning system—the entire system learns which specific strategies are most related to the system's priorities.

One common objection to giving schools the freedom to select their own indicators is the assumption that anarchy and chaos will result. If every school in a ten-school district chooses its own indicators, it would be possible to have sixty separate indicators—an impossible mess! Although theoretically possible, I would offer two observations. First, if there are ten schools, there are probably a lot more than sixty separate initiatives already the central office may or may not know about. Second, when each cause indicator is visibly related to an effect indicator, it will become quickly apparent which of the cause indicators are effective and which are not. For example, some districts engage in the expensive and time-consuming process of curriculum audits. The district evaluates classroom instruction based on the degree to which the teachers deliver the planned curriculum. Although this sounds reasonable enough, there is too often an unanswered question: Do the teachers with the greatest implementation of the curriculum have the greatest gains in student achievement? Certainly, that is the assumption underlying curriculum audits—better implementation means higher achievement. But in my reviews of the data, sometimes that is true and sometimes it is not. Indeed, in one analysis of a mathematics curriculum audit, the teachers who scored lower on curriculum implementation had greater gains in mathematics achievement, and teachers with the highest scores on curriculum implementation had lower gains. It turns out the teachers with lower scores on curriculum implementation were not indifferent or lazy, but rather had a very firm grounding in the curriculum requirements. They also had a very clear understanding of their students' needs and knew to conduct a daily brief preassessment to determine the extent to which students could address the planned lesson. If, for example, the lesson of the day addressed scale and ratio (common requirements in sixth- and seventh-grade mathematics), then it was necessary for the teachers to conduct a quick preassessment to determine if the students had the requisite division and multiplication skills to solve scale and ratio problems. If they did not, then teachers took a quick diversion into the necessary skill building. Although this technique led to better student performance, observers noted the teachers failed to deliver the scale and ratio lesson as planned. To be clear, I support without question the need for a guaranteed and viable curriculum. I also support the need for skillful and effective teaching, a big part of which is making on-the-fly adjustments in a lesson to meet the students' needs.

One of the most overlooked parts of accountability systems is the role of central office departments—transportation, human resources, food service, finance, and so on. In Wayne Township in Indiana, these central office departments report the relationship of their work to districtwide objectives. For example, the transportation department finds on-time bus rides that were discipline-free associated with schools that had better reading performance. By *discipline-free*, the district means that the bus drivers do not refer any behavioral problems to the principal at the conclusion of the bus ride. While the behavior of students on the bus is rarely perfect, a good relationship with the driver can reduce fights and other unsafe behaviors along the route. There is a correlation, though not necessarily a causal relationship, between better bus behavior and higher reading scores. It is not unreasonable, however, to hypothesize that students who are in reading class rather than in the principal's office awaiting their consequence for poor bus behavior might have more reading instruction and subsequently perform better on reading tests. When the human resources (HR) department maintains an effective pipeline of hard-to-find specialties (such as teachers with expertise in special education, English language learning, science, and mathematics), then students perform better. Everyone knows having highly qualified teachers is related to improved student results, but very few accountability systems give the HR department the credit it deserves for making this happen. Moreover, the administration notices the HR department, along with counterparts in safety and finance, primarily when things go wrong—the unlawful termination lawsuit, the avoidable playground accident, or the failed audit. When central office employees are included in a learning system, stakeholders notice these avoided costs—the work done to *avoid* a mistake, rather than just the mistakes themselves.

The third component of a learning system is to identify *a qualitative description*— typically just a page for each school and department—that links the effective variables with the cause variables and provides the story behind the numbers. Although effective accountability relies mainly on quantitative measurements, the truth is there is always a qualitative lens through which they can better understand quantitative data. In chapter 17 (page 161), we will consider examples of these narrative reports.

Summary

In this chapter, we considered the link between equity and excellence schools and effective accountability systems. If you want to find not only your own high-performing, high-poverty schools but also the professional and leadership practices that led to great performance, you must have an accountability system that is more than test scores. Only when an accountability system links *effects* (achievement, attendance, safety, and so on) with *causes* (the actions of teachers and leaders) can accountability become a learning system rather than an instrument to threaten and humiliate teachers and administrators. The components of a learning system include systemwide indicators, school- and department-based indicators, and a narrative explaining the story behind the numbers. In the next chapter, we will consider how to develop systemwide indicators that bring focus and meaning to the goals and priorities of the governing board and senior leadership team.

CHAPTER 15

Enact System-Level Accountability

In this chapter, we will delve into three aspects of system-level accountability: (1) *focus*, (2) *accuracy*, and (3) *specificity*. We begin by discussing how leaders align accountability indicators, strategic plans, and board goals to focus system-level accountability. We will then illustrate the importance of accuracy in system-level indicators by presenting examples of why all educators must understand what the indicators represent. Next, we demonstrate the need for specificity in the language of the indicators, to ensure all stakeholders are on the same page. Finally, we will present an analogy of change involving a rider, an elephant, and a path, and consider what this means for readers hoping to enact change in their schools and districts.

Aligning Accountability Indicators, Strategic Plans, and Board Goals

It is not unusual to find a large number of planning documents in a complex and challenging school, district, or educational system. This is particularly true of high-poverty schools where staff members, trying to help, offer an additional plan. A partial list might include the following.

- Strategic plan
- School-improvement plan
- District-improvement plan
- Title I plan

- Literacy plan
- Mathematics plan
- Early childhood plan
- Career-pathway plan

- Board goals
- Superintendent's vision
- Community engagement plan

These plans are just the tip of a very large iceberg. In my review of more than two thousand school plans, there was an individual school with more than 70 priorities and an individual district with more than 240 priorities (Reeves, 2011b). Most of these priorities probably had merit and certainly were born of good intentions. But taken together, they are a formula for frustration. An effective accountability system can bring focus and alignment to every single plan in the system. The filtering mechanism is very clear (Reeves, 2004).

- **Is there a *specific* and *measurable goal* directly tied to the district's highest priorities?** "Improve communication" is not a goal. "Improve from 42 percent of students reading on grade level to 80 percent of students reading on grade level by the end of the current school year" provides a crystal-clear target that everyone in the system can understand.

- **Are there *explicit cause indicators*—specific actions of teachers, leaders, and other adults in the system—linked to the performance of the goal?** For example, does the accountability system monitor the frequency and effectiveness of classroom observations by administrators? Do the accountability indicators include essential teacher practices such as collaborative scoring or the inclusion of nonfiction writing in every subject?

- **Do we have a clear understanding of *what we will stop doing?*** Harvard professor Michael E. Porter (1996) suggests effective strategies are not just about what an organization will do but also about what an organization will *not* do. To stay with a previous example, if a district aspires to nearly double students' reading proficiency, then any other initiative impinging on literacy time is unacceptable. Any professional practices not associated with improved reading performance are discontinued. Teachers and building administrators can probably make a long list of answers to the question, What are the barriers preventing us from improving literacy performance? A well-focused accountability system provides the leverage to remove those barriers. The list of system-level accountability indicators that deserve the attention of the board and senior leadership is brief: safety, academic performance, and attendance might lead the list.

Although school leaders often believe their goals and visions are clear, over time, the accumulation of one goal on top of another can yield a bewildering array of initiatives that compete for time and resources. Many strategic planning processes fail under the weight of good intentions, such as the attempt to include every good idea, particularly those from influential stakeholders, in the plan. But time and resources are a zero-sum game—every minute and every dollar allocated to one idea, however great it may be, is a dollar and minute subtracted from another great idea. Therefore, strategy is not the art of accumulation but rather the art of focus. One easy way to evaluate strategic planning diagrams is to enlist the aid of colleagues who wear reading glasses. If they need spectacles to read your plan, then it's too dense and detailed. Too many excellent visions and compelling missions are lost in a blizzard of details that are unnecessary and distracting.

Whatever the software used to make the designs, complex diagrams convey the illusion of understanding rather than the reality—there are too many initiatives, and the organization is completely unfocused. Even the most well-focused accountability system, however, is of little value if the reported data are inaccurate. This simple objective is more elusive than it sounds.

Understanding What the Indicators Mean

"Do you mean to tell me," the superintendent asked, his face turning red, "that we can't even take attendance? That we don't know how many students are showing up for school?" After some hesitation, the response from building principals and central office staffers was essentially, "Yes. We have no consistent or coherent policy on taking attendance." It turned out this most simple of metrics—who came to school today—was more ambiguous than it appeared. The gatekeeper for the data in most schools is the administrative assistant, and, in very large schools, someone whose exclusive duty is to be the attendance clerk. But no matter the size of the school, the most consistent element of attendance data is inconsistency. For example, some students are counted as present if they are in school during the first hour of the morning, but absent for the rest of the day. Other students are counted absent if they are not present in the first hour, but then are present for the remainder of the day. Some schools use fractional attendance numbers, so if a student is present for half the day, he or she is counted as half present and half absent. Other schools take an all-or-nothing approach.

Inaccuracy does not simply pertain to attendance. Electronic gradebooks have caused chaos in answering the simple question, What percentage of our students are passing the class? Within the same district, and even within the same schools, there are widely varying protocols for entering student performance data. In some cases, teachers enter assessment data all at once—if a student takes a twenty-item test, then the results on that test are there for all students. But in an adjacent classroom, the teacher might test only five items at a time, so when someone asks, "What percentage of students are passing the class" the answer is zero if the teacher has only implemented five or ten items on a twenty-item test. Some teachers use traditional A, B, C, D, F grading, where A = 4, B = 3, C = 2, D = 1, and F = 0. But other teachers in the same school use A = 90, B = 80, C = 70, D = 60, F = 0. Such inconsistencies are completely chaotic and make the pretense of instructional leadership a hollow claim because the instructional leader has no idea of the success and failure rates of students.

Discipline—something many leaders and board members care deeply about—is wildly inconsistent; two schools with identical disciplinary challenges can report wildly different results. One school reports 300 disciplinary infractions, and the other reports 50. How could they have the same challenges? Because in the first, 250 of the 300 reported infractions are for such conduct as *disrespect* or *incomplete work*, with just 50 for infractions requiring disciplinary interventions. But in the culture of that school, anything displeasing the teacher is recorded as misconduct. In the second school, there is a culture of classroom responsibility, and classroom issues—such as disrespect and incomplete work—are handled in the classroom, and only severe violations are reported as disciplinary infractions.

In sum, it is not enough to create an accountability indicator. Leaders must be specific and consistent in how they measure those indicators at every level, from the classroom to the office of school administrators and the central office.

Establishing Specificity in the Indicators

One of the best books on change, *Switch: How to Change When Change Is Hard*, tells the story of a systematic approach to reducing unnecessary deaths in hospitals (Heath & Heath, 2010). While many people want change—or at least a change in the results, such as reduced deaths—fewer people are enthusiastic about the steps toward change. As the Heath brothers (2010) suggest, it is not enough to have a change initiative—organizations also need to be able to track the degree to which changes are implemented and the results that they achieve. While everyone knows mistakes happen, there had not previously been a quantified approach to identifying the problem, specifying the solution, and measuring results. In introducing a program of six interventions hospitals would implement, the leader provided a clear target (saving one hundred thousand lives) and a date (eighteen months). Note this was not a 150-point strategic plan but just six clear changes and two clear outcomes. Noting the clarity of this goal, the leader said, "*Some* is not a number; *soon* is not a time." This phrase should be imprinted as a watermark on every plan.

Specificity is valuable not only for adults managing large and complex systems but also for students. This is why scoring rubrics written in student-friendly language are so important. When I observe classrooms, I quietly whisper to a student just two questions: "What are we doing?" and "What comes next?" The gold standard answer is, "I'm working on writing my persuasive essay. I need to redo it because I only got a 2, but I know if I add some more evidence to support my claim and have some better transitions between paragraphs, I can get a 3 next time." These questions work well with second and third graders, and I would suggest leaders ask them more frequently in board, cabinet, faculty, grade-level, and department meetings. "What are we doing?" seems like a fair question, but in an extraordinary number of meetings— those without an agenda or purpose but are just a mind-numbing recurrence on the calendar—the honest answer is, "I don't know—I didn't call this meeting." "What comes next?" yields similar blank stares, and the participants' post-meeting discussions in the hallway afterward betray the obscurity or that participants have vastly different understandings about decisions made or not made. Organization practices experts Michael Mankins and Eric Garton (2017) provide evidence of how *organizational drag* undermines the effectiveness of organizations large and small. This research is particularly resonant in high-poverty schools, in which the sources of organizational energy or organizational drag—time, talent, and energy—are particularly important. I regularly consult with principals in high-poverty schools who know that they need to be spending time in classrooms and hallways, but fully 40 percent of their time is consumed in mandatory meetings outside of the building. I work with teachers who know that they need to be engaged in collaborative team meetings to support their professional learning communities, but the majority of that planned meeting time is diverted into one mandatory workshop after another, few of which are related to their mission of serving students. The talent of the organizational drag equation is particularly relevant to high-poverty schools, particularly in systems in which great teachers who are committed to their profession can use seniority rules to move away from schools that most need them. As mentioned earlier in this book, high-poverty schools have the highest turnover rates of leaders and teachers (Reeves, 2018), leaving students to pay the cost of inconsistent teaching and leadership. Individual and organizational energy is squandered because the direction is unclear, and leaders fail to have the courage to make bold and consistent decisions.

Considering the Rider, the Elephant, and the Path as Elements of Change

Change without accountability is mere rhetoric. Best-selling authors Chip and Dan Heath (2013) conclude the three elements of change are (1) *the rider* (the person who sets direction and goals), (2) *the elephant* (the organization the leader is attempting to guide), and (3) *the path*. The Heath brothers (2013) conclude that most change efforts focus only on the rider—the great leader who thinks he is riding a white horse but is, in fact, astride an elephant. It is the third element of change—the path—most likely to guide the elephant. In the context of accountability systems, it is the specification of a few indicators at the system level that sets the path. Sprawling organizations can divert leadership energy in many different ways, and leaders who burden strategic plans with scores—even hundreds—of indicators are riding an elephant while entering a forest without a clear path. Effective accountability systems have not only the goals of the rider and the energy of the elephant but also a clear path to guide both rider and elephant, no matter how difficult the terrain.

Summary

For system-level accountability to be effective, leaders must focus the indicators. Just as the path guided elephants since ancient times, a modern airliner has dozens of indicators for the many systems that guide the airplane, but even the most experienced pilot cannot focus on more than a few of them. These indicators typically include airspeed, attitude (the orientation of the aircraft relative to the horizon), fuel level, and traffic in the vicinity. But none of those gauges will help the pilot if the information is inaccurate. An accountability system is only as good as the accuracy of the information it produces. For system-level indicators to have meaning, plans must be specific, with measurable and time-bound goals. Finally, the accountability system must include the three elements of change—the rider (leader), elephant (organization), and the path (to successful change). In the context of education, the path may be different from one school or department to another. The level of accountability is where we next turn our attention.

CHAPTER 16

Enact School- and Department- Level Accountability

This chapter begins with a discussion of school- and department-level account-ability and how leaders can customize lower-level indicators while maintaining overall clarity. We will then consider how to measure and test both teaching and leadership practices as part of a hypothesis. Finally, this chapter will remind readers of the importance of considering central office departments, such as human resources and even the transportation system, within school-level performance indicators and their impact on student performance.

Moving From Chaos to Clarity

The first level of accountability system design is having system-level indicators that provide focus and clarity for the entire system. The second level of accountability allows for different indicators for the varying needs of each school and central office department. The idea of different indicators for different schools will strike many people as an invitation to chaos. Moreover, when considering system-level indicators and emphasizing the need for focus, this appears to invite just the opposite. So, let me offer some important clarifications.

First, everyone in the system—every school and every central office department—focuses on the same system-level goals: safety, academic achievement, attendance, and so on. But the ways to accomplish these goals may be quite different. Consider the issue of academic achievement. In some schools where students arrive performing at grade level, have the support of over-involved parents, and go home to houses full of books, the mere delivery of the curriculum may be sufficient. But for equity and excellence schools, the vast majority of the support students receive will be during the school day. There is no presumption of homework, after-school or before-school activities, or weekend cram sessions. All these schools have are the hours in the school day, so school-based accountability indicators must focus on more than the mere delivery of the curriculum. These schools do not measure indicators only once, but rather, as the following examples suggest, throughout the year so the faculty sees growth. Examples of school-based indicators might include the following.

- Percentage of teachers that leaders rate as effective or highly effective in instructional delivery after monthly mini-observations (It is important to distinguish these classroom observations that are focused on actual teacher performance from formal end-of-year evaluations that tend to be far less helpful. The informal observations can state honestly that fewer than half the students were engaged, or that the teacher failed to intervene and support students who clearly were not participating in the lesson. The end-of-year evaluations, by contrast, typically regard almost all teachers as satisfactory or better. Thus, the informal observations, not end-of-year evaluations, are far better indicators for a learning system.)

- Percentage of teachers that leaders rate as effective or highly effective in classroom management after monthly mini-observations

- Percentage of teachers that leaders rate as effective or highly effective in lesson planning after monthly reviews

- Percentage of teachers that leaders rate as effective or highly effective in professional responsibilities after monthly mini-observations

- Frequency of nonfiction writing

- Frequency and accuracy of collaborative scoring of student work

- Frequency of cross-disciplinary student assignments

- Accuracy of student self-assessment

- Frequency of student collaboration (based on the accuracy of student comments on the work of peers)

- Percentage of collaborative team meetings that address the four critical PLC questions within a month
- Percentage of students engaged in team or class leadership opportunities

The challenge remains: if every school chooses different indicators, then there will be so many indicators that accountability will dissolve into a chaotic mess. But in reality, that chaos turns into order very quickly. A three-year observation of one complex accountability system finds 135 schools had the opportunity to choose up to six school-based indicators. Theoretically, this could have led to more than eight hundred indicators. In fact, in the first year, there were a total of ninety-nine indicators. Because the relationship between school-based indicators and system-level results is transparent, principals could easily observe which were the most powerful school-based indicators. Thus, by the second year, the total number of indicators shrank to sixty, and by the third year, thirty-three. This number is large enough to accommodate the varying needs of different schools and still allow the system to conduct systematic analysis.

Measuring Teaching and Leadership Practices

The most common objection to school-based accountability indicators is that they present an attempt to elevate the *science* of teaching over the *art* of teaching. You cannot measure relationships, critics contend. Although this may be true, you absolutely can measure the antecedents of good relationships. For example, the warmth of a greeting may be ineffably sublime, but there is no hope of that greeting happening if the teachers and administrators do not know students' names. Therefore, measure the degree to which teachers know the names and pictures of students and at least one thing about each student outside his or her schoolwork. Leaders can systematically observe the degree to which teachers are in the hallway during passing periods, greeting students by name and during in-class interactions, when teachers call on students by name, and encourage and respect them. This is one reason the traditional practice of raising hands to offer an answer is detrimental to classroom engagement. When a student raises a hand to answer a question, it allows other students to check out and remain silent, often for days or weeks at a time. Moreover, hand-raising allows teachers to call on students without knowing their names. By contrast, when teachers must call on students by name, every student is equally engaged, and teachers must know—or at least learn through trial and error—the names of the students in their classes.

Similarly, leaders can measure teaching effectiveness in instructional delivery, classroom management, assessment and feedback, lesson planning, and other areas by using a very specific and consistent rubric. The best ones are free (see Kim Marshall's at https://marshallmemo.com). You can measure the percentage of students who receive feedback from the teacher and the percentage of students who respond to that feedback, as I always do during classroom observations. You can also measure the number of writing portfolios showing evidence of feedback and rewriting, and specified teaching and leadership practices. Leaders should evaluate each staff meeting's productivity and relevance to schoolwide goals. Leaders can measure how frequently principals are in classrooms and how quickly they provide feedback to those they observe. Principals can also measure the extent to which they provide teachers with the opportunity to observe their peers. None of these observations require guesswork, and each data point can be as specific as a test score.

Testing Hypotheses at the School Level

The value of school-based indicators when combined with system-level indicators is that leaders can systematically test hypotheses. Does greater implementation of the curriculum lead to better performance? Does improved lesson planning lead to better student performance? Do personal calls from staff (rather than robocalls) improve attendance? Does collaborative scoring of student work improve the work quality? Will restorative justice improve school discipline? The answers to these questions are not based on external authority, but on observations in local classrooms with local students. Even though I would stake my life on the fact that, for example, improved grading systems lead to better achievement, discipline, and culture, it is like having an argument with the elephant, who is distinctly unimpressed by my statistics. The metaphorical elephant is immovable and unpersuadable. It represents the parents who think on-time attendance is unnecessary, the administrators who believe that their coaching of teachers is less important than paperwork in the office, and the teachers who, in a matter of seconds, have decided the potential of each student. Indeed, sometimes the elephants are the students themselves who seem impervious to teaching because a year or two earlier they decided that they were just not very good at reading. When, by contrast, I create an environment in which teachers can collaboratively test my assertions about grading practices and come to their own conclusions, then I have prepared the path. Circumstances change. Classrooms and schools are different. What works for one school may not work for another. But the essence of school-based accountability indicators is that we must, year in and year out, compare our professional practices with student results.

Remembering Central Office Departments

Central office department personnel are often derided as "just administrators"—until a paycheck is missing, the computer network goes down, the broken windows aren't fixed, the buses are late, or the food is toxic. These departments are noticed primarily when things go wrong. That's too bad, because the hardworking professionals in payroll, technology, maintenance, transportation, and other areas help achieve systemwide accountability indicators and should be recognized for doing so. For example, when teachers complain that students are exhausted and inattentive after lunch, some schools address this concern with lighter and healthier lunch options. When teachers complain that students are late in the morning, some schools adopt monthly recognition of bus drivers who arrive on time and without disciplinary incidents on the bus. Technology is critically important in every school, yet computers and networks break down. One system measures the *ticket time*—that is, the number of minutes that elapse from a request for service from the technology department to the resolution of the request. When this department posted the ticket time results visibly, this same staff with the same resources dramatically decreased the turnaround time for technology support requests. Everyone would agree that teaching and leadership quality is essential for effective education and the achievement of systemwide indicators, but the evidence suggests that the teacher pipeline is declining (Reeves, 2018). Some HR departments mentor and publicly post their pipeline results, especially in hard-to-fill teaching positions such as those in special education, mathematics, and science. The same elements of focus, accuracy, and specificity that pertain to system and school objectives also characterize the most effective department accountability indicators.

Summary

School and department accountability indicators are at the heart of what makes accountability systems work. They are the objectively measurable actions of adults so important in leading the accomplishments of students. Whether the objective is attendance, academic achievement, or behavior, there are adult actions behind every objective. When we fail to measure and report publicly on these objectives, the explanations for failure are left to conjecture. "It's just those students. It's their families. It's their neighborhoods." But that default explanation becomes untenable when there is evidence from schools and classrooms with the same student demographics that show success. The difference is not the students, but the adults, and effective accountability systems allow us to take responsibility and give credit where it is due.

Although this chapter maintains the conviction that we should measure much of adult performance and link it to student results, it is also true there are elements of schools and department operations that require a qualitative rather than quantitative explanation. That is the subject of the next chapter.

CHAPTER 17

Explain the Story Behind the Numbers

An effective accountability system has three parts: (1) system-level indicators that reflect the goals common throughout the system, (2) school and department indicators that reflect the specific actions of teachers and administrators to help their school or department achieve the system-level indicators, and (3) brief narratives that help stakeholders understand the relationships among the first two parts of the system. This chapter will help educators understand the third of these three elements: *the narrative behind the numbers*. It begins with an example of a clear, concise narrative that quickly sums up the factors affecting the data while highlighting only a couple relevant indicators of the many for a particular school. It then discusses two benefits of narrative writing: (1) the ability to provide an explanation for tragedies and triumphs affecting the data, and (2) the possibility of helping parents, policymakers, and members of the community by encouraging continued involvement in schools. Such narratives provide support not only to those seeking to understand the data but also to the students themselves.

Writing a Narrative

The narrative aspect of an effective accountability system helps stakeholders understand the relationships between the system-level indicators and the school- or department-level indicators. In essence, the *narrative* explains the story behind the numbers. Tragedies, such as the death or serious illness of a student or faculty member, can influence performance. Or, the student population may have unique characteristics a reader of the document should understand to make the most accurate possible interpretation of the data. A narrative provides the qualitative data necessary to most fully understand the effectiveness of equity and excellence practices recommended in this book.

I recommend the narrative be brief—not longer than a page—and expressed in language that parents, colleagues, community and board members, and other policymakers can easily understand.

For example, a middle-school narrative might read as follows.

The Monroe Mustangs enjoyed another great year of learning. Our state test scores show only slight gains from the previous year, but we have gathered additional data showing that for the students who were with us for the full school year, gains in reading averaged 1.5 grade levels and gains in mathematics averaged 1.8 grade levels. What accounts for the difference between the relatively small gains in state tests and our tremendous internal gains? We believe there are two factors at work. First, because of the neighboring state prison, a substantial number of our families are transient—more than half of the students who took the test in April were not in our classrooms from September through December. We are certainly responsible for every student for every day he or she is here, but it is not surprising that students who are here for nine months make more progress than those who are here for only two. Second, while our intervention programs have been very successful, they have the greatest impact when we can schedule students for appropriate interventions based on accurate incoming data. We have learned that many students come to us with records displaying satisfactory performance, but after a month in our classes, it's clear these students are several years behind their peers. In order to address this, we began a new system to assess every incoming student, and, without regard to his or her previous transcripts, we assign these students immediately to appropriate intervention programs.

An analysis of our building-level accountability indicators reveals the positive impact our teaching strategies have had on student learning. Compared to the previous year, we have tripled the amount of nonfiction writing our students are doing, including writing consistently about claims and evidence not only in English language arts but also in science and social studies. Our growing population of English language learners especially enjoyed the opportunity to debate topics of interest to them, which ranged from comparisons of international food preferences to immigration policies. These debates not only helped our students express themselves but also helped model the civil discourse and disagreement that we know will help them in high school and throughout their lives.

Finally, our school-based indicators identified some things we were doing that did not live up to our expectations. Our student discipline data were very similar to the previous year, and the new discipline program, for which all staff were trained, appeared to have no impact. We are taking this evidence to heart as we redesign our discipline program from the ground up. We will shift our focus from consequences to personal responsibility through our "Every Mustang Matters" campaign. This will include peer counseling and support rather than merely a discipline program exclusively focused on teachers and administrators as enforcers.

Note the school had six system-level indicators and six school-based indicators, but only addressed a few of them in the narrative. Moreover, the school's internal formative data showed growth not part of the system-level indicators, but the principal and faculty believed their own formative data provided necessary context for understanding the system-level data. Certainly, teachers and administrators could write many pages explaining data, but my experience is that the length of an explanation is inversely related to its readership. If we want parents, policymakers, and the public to understand our schools, we need to keep the report brief and focused.

Writing Narratives to Provide an Explanation for Triumphs and Tragedies

I worked in a school in which the principal was, of course, terminated because mathematics scores were too low. However, over the course of the single year prior to the principal's termination, a student was murdered, another student died on the bus, a parent was murdered, and more than a third of the children in the school were homeless. The students came from dangerous homes in gang-controlled neighborhoods. Within feet of the school grounds, there were drug deals and gang fights. The teachers at this school did more than cover the curriculum; they fed, bathed, and washed clothes of these students. I don't know if a narrative would have prevented this mindless administrative action, but at least it would have provided some context for the numbers.

There are also great triumphs we should celebrate in schools, but which exclusive emphasis on quantitative data obscures. For example, a middle school mathematics team did such a great job in sixth and seventh grades that an exceptionally high number of eighth-grade students took the ninth-grade algebra test. That led to eighth-grade average scores plummeting because the highest-achieving students did not take the eighth-grade test. Rather than assuming mathematics teachers are incompetent, readers of a narrative would understand the context and celebrate the achievement of these great teachers and students.

Writing Narratives to Benefit Parents and Policymakers

Schools and society benefit when parents decide to send their children to public schools. Although many independent schools and some charter schools provide excellent educational opportunities, the supply is limited only to a few self-selected families and students. The well-known *Matthew Effect* is based on the verse from the Bible's Gospel of Matthew that reads: "For to everyone who has will more be given, and he will have abundance; but from him who has not, even what he has will be taken away" (Matthew 25:29, Revised Standard Version). There are similar verses in Mark and Luke. Certainly, the Matthew Effect applies to schools; those schools with the highest-achieving students and best teachers attract even more high-achieving students and top teachers. For the vast majority of families, however, regular public schools are the only option, and effective accountability systems must focus on how to make these schools successful.

Many jurisdictions do not have school boundaries, so parents can send their children to any school in the district. In some U.S. states, parents can choose schools in different districts. If all parents see is the typical report card school ratings, they might understandably move their children from a *C* school to an *A* school. The result is that students who have attentive and engaged parents move out of struggling schools into schools already performing well. This skimming effect perpetuates a system in which middle- and low-achieving students are rarely, if ever, exposed to the academic rigor and high expectations accorded to their high-achieving peers. In a study of valedictorians in Massachusetts (as cited in Walker, 2019), researchers find an enormous gap between the *exam schools* (which limit admission to students who achieve the highest marks on a sixth-grade test) and traditional high schools. While top students in urban exam schools and suburban schools had successful college careers and achieved many of their career ambitions, the top students in non-exam urban schools received academic acclaim, but little else. Few students in the latter category graduated from college in four years. Although 40 percent of these students aspired to be doctors, none earned a medical degree. Therefore, who could blame a parent or student from shunning traditional public schools? This is where an effective accountability system comes in. When accountability systems are based solely on scores, the Matthew Effect will doom almost any chances for improvement. But when an accountability system tells the whole story, including not only test scores but also the story behind the numbers, then parents can make an informed choice that their traditional public school might be far better than the letter grades make it appear.

This phenomenon is true in urban areas as well as in the rural heartland, where declining student populations make it much more difficult to maintain the curricula and teaching professionals essential for schools to meet all state or provincial requirements. As more rural schools consolidate in the name of efficiency and in pursuit of higher scores in traditional accountability systems, the resulting two-hour bus rides for the remaining rural residents are difficult to associate with improved opportunities.

It is vital that explanations of test scores, divulging tragedies and triumphs, are not presented as excuses for low performance. They are, rather, a means for policymakers to prepare the path, providing insights and information parents and students can use to make the best possible decision. From a policymaker's perspective, this sort of comprehensive information provides the nuances and understanding essential to make the best possible decisions about resource allocation, as well as decisions to renew or close schools.

Summary

Quantification of student performance is important, but it does not tell the whole story. Schools do not need an encyclopedic explanation of data, but they do need to provide a brief narrative explaining the relationship between system-level indicators and specific actions of professionals at the school. Moreover, schools need the opportunity to acknowledge what does not work and plan improvements accordingly. And, without making excuses, schools deserve the opportunity to help parents and policymakers understand that the story of their school and the students they serve have a context that numbers alone never tell.

Giant Leaps,
Not Baby Steps

Since the original publication of the equity and excellence research (Reeves, 2004), schools and districts have widely replicated these practices, with other researchers finding similar results. Education writer Karin Chenoweth (2009); the Education Trust (n.d.); Zavadsky (2009); University of Mississippi graduate student Aubrey Womack, professor Jerilou J. Moore, and professor P. Renee Hill-Cunningham (2018), and many others contribute to this growing body of research. Many more were cited in the introduction of this book and do not require repetition here. Although I hope you will share this book and the work of other researchers I have cited with your colleagues, community and board members, legislators, and anyone else willing to read it, I know this is certain: *evidence is not enough.* Although there is plentiful evidence showing high performance in high-poverty schools is possible and doesn't require a change in budget, union agreement, or schedule, many initiative-weary educators are resistant to changes they believe will not work in their schools. Implementing equity and excellence principles in a way that gives students from economically disadvantaged families the opportunities they deserve will require actions that matter, not just words.

There was a time in U.S. history when, as a matter of philosophy and religion, there was a widespread presumption that the poor deserved their fate. The doctrine of *predestination,* in at least some interpretations, suggests both our earthly and heavenly lot is determined before we are born. Just as poverty was a just punishment inflicted on the undeserving, wealth was an equally just reward (Basinger & Basinger, 1986). Accepting the poor as doomed to their fate was not only good theology in colonial days but also good economics. Economist and demographer Thomas Malthus provides academic cover for disdain for the poor (as cited in Thoma, 2006). Writing in the late 18th century, Malthus finds a ready audience already disposed to detest the poor:

> A man who is born into a world already possessed, if he cannot get subsistence from his parents on whom he has a just demand, and if the society do not want his labor, has no claim of right to the smallest portion of food, and, in fact, has no business to be where he is. At nature's mighty feast there is no vacant cover for him. (as cited in Thoma, 2006)

There are echoes of this philosophy even today, in infomercials promising if only they work hard enough and believe sincerely enough, the poor can achieve the prosperity which eludes them.

The question as I close this book is this: Have we learned anything in the past three centuries? Whenever I hear the poor, from kindergarteners to their great-grandparents, consigned to the scrap heap of despair, I wonder how in three hundred years we could learn so much about science and medicine and so little about poverty and the human condition. If the years ahead are to be different, it will be because people like you choose to transform words into deeds, and philosophy into action. The challenge is not one of incrementalism or timid baby steps by those who fear the loss of popularity more than the loss of young lives. The challenge is for giant leaps. When you read about a goal of moving a school from 20 percent of students reading on grade level to 22 percent, you are witnessing 21st century predestination in which 78 percent of students are ordained to the lifelong burden of illiteracy and failure.

There is a better vision calling us! The students, teachers, leaders, and parents of equity and excellence schools do not wait for new legislation, new budgets, new strategic plans, or another raft of new programs. They put a laser-like focus on student achievement *right now.* Students are tired of waiting; we owe it to them to take up the challenge.

References and Resources

Ablon, J. S. (2018). *Changeable: How collaborative problem solving changes lives at home, at school, and at work.* New York: Penguin.

Ainsworth, L. (2004). *Power standards: Identifying the standards that matter the most.* Englewood, CO: Advanced Learning Press.

Ainsworth, L., & Viegut, D. (2006). *Common formative assessments: How to connect standards-based instruction and assessment.* Thousand Oaks, CA: Corwin Press.

Alliance for Excellent Education. (n.d.). *Every child a graduate; every child prepared for life.* Accessed at All4ed.org on September 16, 2019.

Allison, E., & Reeves, D. B. (2012). *Renewal coaching fieldbook: How effective leaders sustain meaningful change.* San Francisco: Jossey-Bass.

Angelou, M. (1969). *I know why the caged bird sings.* New York: Random House.

Baldwin, J. (2011). *Fifty famous stories retold.* Overland Park, KS: Digireads.

Bambrick-Santoyo, P. (2018). *Leverage leadership 2.0: A practical guide to building exceptional schools* (2nd ed.). San Francisco: Jossey-Bass.

Basinger, D., & Basinger, R. (Eds.). (1986). *Predestination & free will: Four views of divine sovereignty & human freedom.* Downers Grove, IL: InterVarsity Press.

Bleier, E. (2019, January 28). Vince Lombardi: What he said to his team and what they said about him. *Inside Hook.* Accessed at www.insidehook.com/article/sports/vince-lombardi-said-said on September 16, 2019.

Blinder, A. (2015, April 1). Atlanta educators convicted in school cheating scandal. *New York Times.* Accessed at https://nytimes.com/2015/04/02/us/verdict-reached-in-atlanta-school-testing-trial.html on July 9, 2019.

Brenneman, R. (2016, March 22). Gallup student poll finds engagement in school dropping by grade level. *Education Week, 35*(25), 6.

Brown, B. (2018). *Dare to lead: Brave work, tough conversations, whole hearts.* New York: Random House.

Buckingham, M., & Coffman, C. (1999). *First, break all the rules: What the world's greatest managers do differently.* New York: Simon & Schuster.

Burns, D. D. (1980). *Feeling good: The new mood therapy.* New York: Morrow.

California State Board of Education. (2019). *Content standards.* Accessed at www.cde .ca.gov/be/st/ss/on September 16, 2019.

Calkins, L. M. (1983). *Lessons from a child: On the teaching and learning of writing.* Exeter, NH: Heinemann.

Calkins, L. M. (1994). *The art of teaching writing* (New ed.). Portsmouth, NH: Heinemann.

Calkins L. (2019). *Leading well: Building schoolwide excellence in reading and writing.* Portsmouth, NH: Heinemann.

Campbell, A., Whitehead, J., & Finkelstein, S. (2009). Why good leaders make bad decisions. *Harvard Business Review, 87*(2), 60–66.

Carroll, G. (Producer), & Rosenberg, S. (Director). (1967). *Cool hand Luke* [Motion picture]. United States: Warner Brothers.

Chenoweth, K. (2007). *It's being done: Academic success in unexpected schools.* Cambridge, MA: Harvard Education Press.

Chenoweth, K. (2009). *How it's being done: Urgent lessons from unexpected schools.* Cambridge, MA: Harvard Education Press.

Chenoweth, K. (2017). *Schools that succeed: How educators marshal the power of systems for improvement.* Cambridge, MA: Harvard Education Press.

Chenoweth, K. (2019). *ExtraOrdinary districts special edition: The Milford 11.* Accessed at https://edtrust.org/the-equity-line/extraordinary-districts-special-edition-the-milford-11/ on September 27, 2019.

Chenoweth, K., & Theokas, C. (2011). *Getting it done: Leading academic success in unexpected schools.* Cambridge, MA: Harvard Education Press.

Childress, S. M., Doyle, D. P., & Thomas, D. A. (2009). *Leading for equity: The pursuit of excellence in Montgomery County Public Schools.* Cambridge, MA: Harvard Education Press.

Clear, J. (2018). *Atomic habits: Tiny changes, remarkable results—An easy & proven way to build good habits & break bad ones.* New York: Avery.

Coleman, J. S., Campbell, E. Q., Hobson, C. J., McPartland, J., Mood, A. M., Weinfeld, F. D., et al. (1966). *Equality of educational opportunity* [Survey]. Washington, DC: National Center for Educational Statistics.

Collins, J., & Hansen, M.T. (2011). *Great by choice: Uncertainty, chaos, and luck—Why some thrive despite them all.* New York: HarperCollins.

Crenshaw, D. (2008). *The myth of multitasking: How doing it all gets nothing done.* San Francisco: Jossey-Bass.

Daskal, L. (2016, March 28). 100 answers to the question: What is leadership? *Inc.* Accessed at www.inc.com/lolly-daskal/100-answers-to-the-question-what-is-leadership.html on July 9, 2019.

DeSteno, D. (2018). *Emotional success: The power of gratitude, compassion, and pride.* Boston: Houghton Mifflin Harcourt.

Deutschman, A. (2007). *Change or die: The three keys to change at work and in life.* New York: Regan.

DeVito, D., Shamberg, M., & Sher, S. (Producers), & LaGravenese, R. (Director). (2007). *Freedom writers* [Motion picture]. United States: Paramount Pictures.

Diener, E., & Biswas-Diener, R. (2019). *The replication crisis in psychology.* Accessed at https://nobaproject.com/modules/the-replication-crisis-in-psychology on September 30, 2019.

Disare, M. (2017, October 10). 97 percent of New York City teachers earn high marks on latest evaluations, union president says. *Chalkbeat.* Accessed at https://chalkbeat.org/posts /ny/2017/10/10/97-percent-of-new-york-city-teachers-earn-high-marks-on-latest-evaluations-union-president-says on July 9, 2019.

Donohoo, J. (2017). *Collective efficacy: How educators' beliefs impact student learning.* Thousand Oaks, CA: Corwin.

DuFour, R., DuFour, R., Eaker, R., & Many, T. W. (2010). *Learning by doing: A handbook for Professional Learning Communities at Work* (2nd ed.). Bloomington, IN: Solution Tree Press.

DuFour, R., DuFour, R., Eaker, R., Many, T. W., & Mattos, M. (2016). *Learning by doing: A handbook for Professional Learning Communities at Work* (3rd ed.). Bloomington, IN: Solution Tree Press.

DuFour, R., & Reeves, D. (2016). The futility of PLC lite. *Phi Delta Kappan, 97*(6), 69–71.

DuFour, R., Reeves, D., & DuFour, R. (2018). *Responding to the Every Student Succeeds Act with the PLC at Work process.* Bloomington, IN: Solution Tree Press.

Dweck, C. S. (2008). *Mindset: The new psychology of success.* New York: Random House.

Eaker, R., & Keating, J. (2015). *Kid by kid, skill by skill: Teaching in a Professional Learning Community at Work.* Bloomington, IN: Solution Tree Press.

Education Trust. (n.d.). *Dispelling the myth.* Accessed at https://edtrust.org/dispelling_the_myth on July 9, 2019.

Egenfeldt-Nielsen, S. (2006). Overview of research on the educational use of video games. *Nordic Journal of Digital Literacy, 1*(3), 184–214.

Eisenstat, R., Spector, B., & Beer, M. (1990). Why change programs don't produce change. *Harvard Business Review, 68*(6), 158–166.

Fisher, M. (2010, April 28). Why the military declared war on PowerPoint. *Atlantic.* Accessed at https://theatlantic.com/politics/archive/2010/04/why-the-military-declared-war-on-power point/345802 on July 9, 2019.

Fullan, M. (2008). *The six secrets of change: What the best leaders do to help their organizations survive and thrive.* San Francisco: Jossey-Bass.

Fullan, M. (2016). *The new meaning of educational change* (5th ed.). New York: Teachers College Press.

Fullan, M., & Pinchot, M. (2018). The fast track to sustainable turnaround. *Educational Leadership, 75*(6), 48–54.

Gabriel, T., Martin, J., & Fandos, N. (2019, January 14). Steve King removed from committee assignments over white supremacy remark. *New York Times.* Accessed at https://nytimes. com/2019/01/14/us/politics/steve-king-white-supremacy.html on July 9, 2019.

Gay, M. (2019a, January 17). The race to get into Boston's exam schools. *Boston Globe.* Accessed at https://apps.bostonglobe.com/magazine/graphics/2019/01/17/valedictorians/exam-school-divide/ on July 9, 2019.

Gay, M. (2019b, January 28). How can it be true? Many valedictorians of Boston public schools struggle to make a middle-class income. *Boston Globe.* Accessed at https://bostonglobe.com/metro/2019/01/28/how-can-true-many-valedictorians-boston-public-schools-struggle-make-middle-class-income/zJW1dZcBbEAvRj0DckgK3M/story.html on July 9, 2019.

Gershoff, E. T., & Font, S. A. (2016). Corporal punishment in U.S. public schools: Prevalence, disparities in use, and status in state and federal policy. *Social Policy Report, 30*(1).

Gillihan, S. J. (2018). *Cognitive behavioral therapy made simple: 10 strategies for managing anxiety, depression, anger, panic, and worry.* Emeryville, CA: Althea Press.

Gould, S. J. (1996). *The mismeasure of man.* New York: Norton.

Graham, S. (2019). Changing how writing is taught. *Review of Research in Education, 34*(1), 277–303.

Grant, A. (2019). *Power moves: Lessons from Davos* [Audiobook]. Accessed at Audible.com.

Guskey, T. R. (2015). *On your mark: Challenging the conventions of grading and reporting.* Bloomington, IN: Solution Tree Press.

Hamilton, L. (2018, May 24). *New report details challenges facing Boston's public high schools* [Blog post]. Accessed at https://barrfoundation.org/blog/new-report-details-challenges-facing-boston-s-public-high-schools on July 9, 2019.

Hargreaves, A., & Fullan, M. (2012). *Professional capital: Transforming teaching in every school.* New York: Teachers College Press.

Hattie, J. A. C. (2009). *Visible learning: A synthesis of over 800 meta-analyses relating to achievement.* London: Routledge.

Hattie, J. (2012). *Visible learning for teachers: Maximizing impact on learning.* London: Routledge.

Heath, C., & Heath, D. (2010). *Switch: How to change when change is hard.* New York: Broadway Books.

Heath, C., & Heath, D. (2013). *Decisive: How to make better choices in life and work.* New York: Crown Business.

Heath, C., & Heath, D. (2017). The power of moments: Why certain experiences have extraordinary impact. *Fast Company.* Accessed at www.fastcompany.com/40472116/the-power-of-moments-why-certain-experiences-have-extraordinary-impact on September 27, 2019.

Hogan, A., Sellar, S., & Lingard, B. (2015). Commercializing comparison: Pearson puts the TLC in soft capitalism. *Journal of Education Policy, 31*(3), 1–16.

Janis, I. L. (1982). *Groupthink: Psychological studies of policy decisions and fiascoes* (2nd ed.). Boston: Houghton Mifflin.

Jenkins, C., & Garcia-Navarro, L. (2018, November 11). The American Academy of Pediatrics on spanking children: Don't do it, ever. *National Public Radio.* Accessed at https://npr.org/2018/11/11/666646403/the-american-academy-of-pediatrics-on-spanking-children-dont-do-it-ever on July 9, 2019.

Johnson, S. M., Reinhorn, S. K., & Simon, N. S. (2018). Ending isolation: The payoff of teacher teams in successful high-poverty urban schools. *Teachers College Record, 120*(5), 1–46.

Killion, J. (2017). Meta-analysis reveals coaching's positive impact on instruction and achievement. *Learning Professional, 38*(2), 20–23.

Korpella, R. (n.d.). How to sister a floor joist. *SFGate.* Accessed at https://homeguides.sfgate.com/sister-floor-joist-42337.html on July 9, 2019.

Kotter, J. P. (1995, May–June). Leading change: Why transformation efforts fail. *Harvard Business Review, 73*(2), 59–67.

Kotter, J. P. (1996). *Leading change.* Boston: Harvard Business School Press.

Kotter, J. P. (2009). Four ways to increase the urgency needed for change. *Harvard Business Review.* Accessed at https://hbr.org/2009/04/four-ways-to-increase-the-urge.html on November 20, 2019.

Kotter, J. P. (2012). *Leading change* (Rev. ed.). Boston: Harvard Business School Press.

Kouzes, J. M., & Posner, B. Z. (2011). *Credibility: How leaders gain and lose it, why people demand it.* San Francisco: Jossey-Bass.

Lafley, A. G., Martin, R. L., Rivkin, J. W., & Siggelkow, N. (2012, September). Bringing science to the art of strategy. *Harvard Business Review.* Accessed at https://hbr.org/2012/09/bringing-science-to-the-art-of-strategy on July 9, 2019.

Lepore, J. (2018). *These truths: A history of the United States.* New York: W. W. Norton.

Levin, S., & Bradley, K. (2019, March 19). Understanding and addressing principal turnover: A review of the research. *Learning Policy Institute.* Accessed at https://learningpolicyinstitute.org/product/nassp-understanding-addressing-principal-turnover-review-research-report on September 16, 2019.

Leyva De Los Rios, C. D. (2017, March 23). Statistical significance vs. clinical significance. *Students 4 Best Evidence.* Accessed at https://www.students4bestevidence.net/blog/2017/03/23/statistical-significance-vs-clinical-significance/ on July 9, 2019.

Lohmann, R. C. (2015, April 6). *Weighing in . . . Should schools assess body mass index (BMI)?* [Blog post]. Accessed at https://psychologytoday.com/us/blog/teen-angst/201504/weighing-in-should-schools-assess-body-mass-index-bmi on July 9, 2019.

Louisiana State University Shreveport. (2018, January 19). *The problem of principal turnover.* Accessed at https://online.lsus.edu/articles/education/problem-of-principal-turnover.aspx on July 9, 2019.

Lundahl, E. (2013, September 26). Less than 2 percent of carpenters are women—Meet the master builder working to change that. *Yes!* Accessed at https://yesmagazine.org/new-economy/less-than-two-percent-of-carpenters-are-women-meet-master-builder on July 9, 2019.

Lynch, J. R., Cunningham, M. R., Warme, W. J., Schaad, D. C., Wolf, F. M., & Leopold, S. S. (2007). Commercially funded and United States–based research is more likely to be published; good-quality studies with negative outcomes are not. *Journal of Bone and Joint Surgery, 89*(5), 1010–1018.

Mail Foreign Service. (2010, April 28). 'When we understand that slide, we'll have won the war:' US generals given baffling PowerPoint presentation to try to explain Afghanistan mess. *Daily Mail*. Accessed at https://dailymail.co.uk/news/article-1269463/Afghanistan-PowerPoint-slide-Generals-left-baffled-PowerPoint-slide.html on July 9, 2019.

Mankins, M., & Garton, E. (2017). *Time, talent, energy: Overcome organizational drag and unleash your team's productive power.* Boston: Harvard Business Review Press.

Marshall, K. (2005). It's time to rethink teacher supervision and evaluation. *Phi Delta Kappan, 86*(10), 727–735. Accessed at https://doi.org/10.1177/003172170508601004 on July 9, 2019.

Marshall, K. (2009). *Rethinking teacher supervision and evaluation: How to work smart, build collaboration, and close the achievement gap.* San Francisco: Jossey-Bass.

Marzano, R. J. (2017). *The new art and science of teaching.* Bloomington, IN: Solution Tree Press.

Marzano, R. J., Norford, J. S., & Ruyle, M. (2019). *The new art and science of classroom assessment.* Bloomington, IN: Solution Tree Press.

Massachusetts Department of Elementary and Secondary Education. (n.d.). *MA Expanded Learning Time (ELT).* Accessed at http://www.doe.mass.edu/redesign/elt on September 16, 2019.

Mazur, E. (1997). *Peer instruction: A user's manual.* Upper Saddle River, NJ: Prentice Hall.

McKibben, S. (2018). Push, don't pity, students in poverty. *Education Update, 60*(1), 1, 4–5.

Milmo, C. (2007, October 17). Fury at DNA pioneer's theory: Africans are less intelligent than Westerners. *Independent*. Accessed at https://independent.co.uk/news/science/fury-at-dna-pioneers-theory-africans-are-less-intelligent-than-westerners-394898.html on July 9, 2019.

Moore, B. (2018, January 10). *Collective efficacy: The holy grail for school improvement* [Blog post]. Accessed at https://epicimpactedgroup.com/blog/2017/9/8/collective-efficacy-the-holy-grail-to-school-improvement on July 9, 2019.

Mueller, P. A., & Oppenheimer, D. M. (2014). The pen is mightier than the keyboard: Advantages of longhand over laptop note taking. *Psychological Science, 25*(6), 1159–1168.

Muhammad, A., & Cruz, L. F. (2019). *Time for change: Four essential skills for transformational school and district leaders.* Bloomington, IN: Solution Tree Press.

Musca, T. (Producer), & Menéndez, R. (Director). (1988). *Stand and deliver* [Motion picture]. United States: Warner Bros.

National Writing Project. (2009, June 19). *Steve Graham on the importance of learning to write well.* Accessed at www.nwp.org/cs/public/print/resource/2901 on July 9, 2019.

New York Times Editorial Board. (2019, March 30). New York's best schools need to do better. *New York Times*. Accessed at www.nytimes.com/2019/03/30/opinion/new-york-specialized-high-schools-black-hispanic.html?searchResultPosition=14 on September 16, 2019.

Paterson, J. (2018). School turnaround requires uprooting deep issues. *Principal Leadership*. Accessed at www.nassp.org/2018/12/01/school-turnaround-requires-uprooting-deep-issues/ on September 27, 2019.

Petrilli, M. J. (2019). The 'left behind' kids made incredible progress from the late 1990s until the Great Recession. Here are key lessons for ed reform. *Thomas B. Fordham Institute.* Accessed at https://fordhaminstitute.org/national/commentary/left-behind-kids-made-incredible-progress-late-1990s-until-great-recession-here on September 27, 2019.

Pettersson, H., & Briggs, K. (2019). *The meeting is dead, long live the meeting.* Accessed at https://fordhaminstitute.org/national/commentary/meeting-dead-long-live-meeting on September 27, 2019.

Phi Delta Kappa International. (2018, August 25). *The 50th annual PDK poll of the public's attitudes toward the public schools.* Accessed at https://kappanonline.org/the-50th-annual-pdk-poll-of-the-publics-attitudes-toward-the-public-schools on July 9, 2019.

Pink, D. H. (2018). *When: The scientific secrets of perfect timing.* New York: Riverhead Books.

Pondiscio, R. (2019). *How the other half learns: Equality, excellence, and the battle over school choice.* New York: Avery.

Porter, M. E. (1996, November–December). What is strategy? *Harvard Business Review, 74*(6), 61–78.

Rath, T. (2007). *Strengths finder 2.0.* New York: Gallup Press.

Reeves, D. B. (2002a). *The daily disciplines of leadership: How to improve student achievement, staff motivation, and personal organization.* San Francisco: Jossey-Bass.

Reeves, D. B. (2002b). *Making standards work: How to implement standards-based assessments in the classroom, school, and district* (3rd ed.). Denver, CO: Advanced Learning Press.

Reeves, D. B. (2004). *Accountability in action: A blueprint for learning organizations* (2nd ed.). Englewood, CO: Advanced Learning Press.

Reeves, D. B. (2006). *The learning leader: How to focus school improvement for better results.* Alexandria, VA: Association for Supervision and Curriculum Development.

Reeves, D. B. (2008a). The learning leder/The extracurricular advantage. *Educational Leadership, 66*(1), 86–87.

Reeves, D. B. (2008b). *Reframing teacher leadership to improve your school.* Alexandria, VA: Association for Supervision and Curriculum Development.

Reeves, D. B. (2009a). *Assessing educational leaders: Evaluating performance for improved individual and organizational results* (2nd ed.). Thousand Oaks, CA: Corwin Press.

Reeves, D. B. (2009b). *Leading change in your school: How to conquer myths, build commitment, and get results.* Alexandria, VA: Association for Supervision and Curriculum Development.

Reeves, D. B. (2011a). *Elements of grading: A guide to effective practice.* Bloomington, IN: Solution Tree Press.

Reeves, D. B. (2011b). *Finding your leadership focus: What matters most for student results.* New York: Teachers College Press.

Reeves, D. B. (2012). The ketchup solution. *American School Board Journal, 189*(7), 35–36.

Reeves, D. B. (2015). *Inspiring creativity and innovation in K–12.* Bloomington, IN: Solution Tree Press.

Reeves, D. B. (2016a). *Elements of grading: A guide to effective practice* (2nd ed.). Bloomington, IN: Solution Tree Press.

Reeves, D. B. (2016b). *FAST grading: A guide to implementing best practices.* Bloomington, IN: Solution Tree Press.

Reeves, D. B. (2017, November 2). *Busting myths about grading* [Blog post]. Accessed at https:// illuminateed.com/blog/2017/11/busting-myths-about-grading on July 9, 2019.

Reeves, D. B. (2018). Seven keys to restoring the teacher pipeline. *Educational Leadership, 75*(8). Accessed at www.ascd.org/publications/educational-leadership/may18/vol75/num08/ Seven-Keys-to-Restoring-the-Teacher-Pipeline.aspx on July 9, 2019.

Reeves, D. B., & Allison, E. (2009). *Renewal coaching: Sustainable change for individuals and organizations.* San Francisco: Jossey-Bass.

Reeves, D. B., & Allison, E. (2010). *Renewal coaching workbook.* San Francisco: Jossey-Bass.

Reeves, D. B., & DuFour, R. (2016, March). The futility of PLC Lite. *Phi Delta Kappan.* Accessed at www.kappanonline.org/the-futility-of-plc-lite/ on September 27, 2019.

Reeves, D. B., & DuFour, R. B. (2018, February). Next generation accountability. *School Administrator.* Accessed at http://my.aasa.org/AASA/Resources/SAMag/2018/Feb18/ ReevesDuFour.aspx on July 9, 2019.

Reeves, D. B., & Eaker, R. (2019). *100-day leaders: Turning short-term wins into long-term success in schools.* Bloomington, IN: Solution Tree Press.

Schmoker, M. (2001). *The results fieldbook: Practical strategies from dramatically improved schools.* Alexandria, VA: Association for Supervision and Curriculum Development.

Schmoker, M. (2011). *Focus: Elevating the essentials to radically improve student learning.* Alexandria, VA: Association for Supervision and Curriculum Development.

Shakespeare, W. (2016). *Richard II.* New York: Simon & Schuster.

Sherman, S., & Freas, A. (2004). The Wild West of executive coaching. *Harvard Business Review, 82*(11), 82–90. Accessed at https://hbr.org/2004/11/the-wild-west-of-executive-coaching on July 9, 2019.

Slavin, R. (2019a). *Achieving breakthroughs in education by transforming effective but expensive approaches to be affordable at scale* [Blog post]. Accessed at https://robertslavinsblog. wordpress.com/2019/08/15/achieving-breakthroughs-in-education-by-transforming-effective-but-expensive-approaches-to-be-affordable-at-scale/ on September 27, 2019.

Slavin, R. (2019b). *Cost-effectiveness of small solutions* [Blog post]. Accessed at https://robertslavinsblog.wordpress.com/2019/08/22/cost-effectiveness-of-small-solutions/ on September 27, 2019.

Sloman, S., & Fernbach, P. (2017). *The knowledge illusion: Why we never think alone.* New York: Riverhead Books.

Smarick, A. (2016). Is 'district' an operative word? *Thomas B. Fordham Institute.* Accessed at https://fordhaminstitute.org/national/commentary/district-operative-word on September 27, 2019.

Sparks, S. D., & Harwin, A. (2016). Corporal punishment use found in schools in 21 states. *Education Week, 36*(1) 1, 16, 18.

State of New Jersey Department of Education. (2016, December). *2014–15 educator evaluation implementation report.* Accessed at https://nj.gov/education/AchieveNJ/ resources/201415AchieveNJImplementationReport.pdf on July 9, 2019.

Stowe, H. B. (2005). *Uncle Tom's cabin.* New York: Dover.

Strauss, V. (2013, October 4). Case study: The false promise of value-added teacher assessment. *Washington Post*. Accessed at https://washingtonpost.com/news/answer-sheet/wp/2013/10/04/case-study-the-false-promise-of-value-added-teacher-assessment/?noredirect=on&utm_term=.a636d1704ff7 on July 9, 2019.

Superville, D. R. (2016, November 15). Few women run the nation's school districts. Why? *Education Week, 36*(13), 10–11.

Thoma, M. (2006, October 21). *Blaming the poor for their poverty* [Blog post]. Accessed at https://economistsview.typepad.com/economistsview/2006/10/blaming_the_poo.html on July 9, 2019.

Turkle, S. (2015). *Reclaiming conversation: The power of talk in a digital age*. New York: Penguin Press.

Varol, O. (2017, September 8). *Facts don't change people's minds. Here's what does* [Blog post]. Accessed at https://heleo.com/facts-dont-change-peoples-minds-heres/16242 on July 9, 2019.

Venkataraman, B. (2019). *The optimist's telescope: Thinking ahead in a reckless age*. New York: Riverhead Books.

Waack, S. (n.d.). Collective teacher efficacy (CTE) according to John Hattie. *Visible Learning*. Accessed at https://visible-learning.org/2018/03/collective-teacher-efficacy-hattie on July 9, 2019.

Walker, A. (2019, January 22). Valedictorians' struggles reflect rising inequity. *Boston Globe*. Accessed at https://bostonglobe.com/metro/2019/01/22/the-fortunes-our-valedictorians-reflect-our-rising-inequity/H4SrpAst9aKSjXThoZ6vzI/story.html on July 9, 2019.

Wammes, J. D., Meade, M. E., & Fernandes, M. A. (2016). The drawing effect: Evidence for reliable and robust memory benefits in free recall. *Quarterly Journal of Experimental Psychology, 69*(9), 1752–1776.

Westinghouse Science Talent Search. (n.d.). *Finalists named in 57th annual Westinghouse Science Talent Search*. Accessed at https://web.archive.org/web/20110528235249/http:/www2.pr newswire.com/cgi-bin/stories.pl?ACCT=104&STORY=%2Fwww%2Fstory%2F1-27-98%2F402104&EDATE= on July 9, 2019.

Wiggins, G. (1998). *Educative assessment: Designing assessments to inform and improve student performance*. San Francisco: Jossey-Bass.

Wiggins, G. (2014, October 10). *A veteran teacher turned coach shadows 2 students for 2 days—A sobering lesson learned* [Blog post]. Retrieved from https://grantwiggins.wordpress.com/2014/10/10/a-veteran-teacher-turned-coach-shadows-2-students-for-2-days-a-sobering-lesson-learned on July 9, 2019.

Wiggins, L., & Smith, S. (2018). *Leveraging data, curriculum, and teacher leadership*. Accessed at www.nassp.org/2018/12/01/role-call-december-2018/ on September 27, 2019.

Willingham, D. (2018, October 29). *Just how polarized are we about reading instruction?* [Blog post]. Accessed at www.danielwillingham.com/daniel-willingham-science-and-education-blog/just-how-polarized-are-we-about-reading-instruction on July 9, 2019.

Womack, A., Moore, J. J., & Hill-Cunningham, P. R. (2018). Exploring traits of high-performing, high-poverty schools. *International Journal for Innovation Education and Research, 6*(5), 33–40.

Young, S. (2017). *Stick with it: A scientifically proven process for changing your life—for good.* New York: HarperCollins.

Zavadsky, H. (2009). *Bringing school reform to scale: Five award-winning urban districts.* Cambridge, MA: Harvard Education Press.

Index

Praise for

Achieving Equity and Excellence:
Immediate Results From the Lessons of High-Poverty, High-Success Schools

"Insightful, reassuring, and empowering, *Achieving Equity and Excellence: Immediate Results From the Lessons of High-Poverty, High-Success Schools* expands on Doug Reeves's original and groundbreaking 90/90/90 research to vividly proclaim the reality that educators serving communities of all backgrounds—in particular, those in poverty—can and must embrace specific actions that are aligned with a preponderance of evidence that, when implemented, produce both equity and excellence for the students they serve."

—Luis F. Cruz
Educational Consultant and Author

"We must have courage and a steadfast, unwavering commitment toward justice in order to address the inequities that exist in education. *Achieving Equity and Excellence* provides us with the tools to bring words into actions."

—Roger León
Superintendent, Newark Public Schools

"I highly endorse Doug Reeves's latest work on equity and excellence. His words come at an opportune time and provide clear guidance on how to ensure that our pursuit of excellence is accompanied by steps toward equity. Doug outlines what an equity mindset looks like and why action is the only true way to differentiate between those who talk about equity and those who will realize it. Further, Doug embodies a passion for equity each and every day."

—Stacy Scott
Author, *Making Equity Work: Releasing Unlimited Possibilities*
for Closing the Achievement Gap in Your School

"Doug Reeves effectively addresses our greatest challenges in instructional practice, educational research, and how we effectively lead schools. His most recent work on equity and excellence exemplifies his commitment to identifying the best research-based practices while keeping the needs of all students at the center of his work. His findings are right on the mark, and his insights are profoundly important for school and district leaders."

—Chip Kimball
Former Superintendent, Singapore American School, and Lake Washington School District, Washington

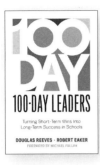

100-Day Leaders
Douglas Reeves and Robert Eaker
Within 100 days, schools can dramatically increase student achievement, transform faculty morale, reduce discipline issues, and much more. Using *100-Day Leaders* as a guide, you will learn how to achieve a series of short-term wins that combine to form long-term success.
BKF919

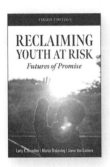

Reclaiming Youth at Risk
Larry K. Brendtro, Martin Brokenleg, and Steve Van Bockernw
Empower your alienated students to cultivate a deep sense of belonging, mastery, independence, and generosity. This fully updated edition of *Reclaiming Youth at Risk* merges Native American knowledge and Western science to create a unique alternative for inspiring troubled youth to thrive and overcome.
BKF914

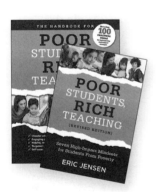

Poor Students, Rich Teaching Bundle
Eric Jensen
You have the power to change the lives of students from poverty. Rely on the new edition of Dr. Eric Jensen's best-selling book *Poor Students, Rich Teaching* and its companion handbook to help you fully embrace the mindsets that lead to richer teaching.
KTF352

Building a Culture of Hope
Robert D. Barr and Emily L. Gibson
Discover a blueprint for turning low-performing schools into *Cultures of Hope*! The authors draw from their own experiences working with high-poverty, high-achieving schools to illustrate how to support students with an approach that considers social as well as emotional factors.
BKF503

a division of

Solution Tree | Press
Solution Tree

Visit SolutionTree.com or call 800.733.6786 to order.

Wait! Your professional development journey doesn't have to end with the last pages of this book.

We realize improving student learning doesn't happen overnight. And your school or district shouldn't be left to puzzle out all the details of this process alone.

No matter where you are on the journey, we're committed to helping you get to the next stage.

Take advantage of everything from **custom workshops** to **keynote presentations** and **interactive web and video conferencing**. We can even help you develop an action plan tailored to fit your specific needs.

Let's get the conversation started.

Call 888.763.9045 today.

SolutionTree.com